FLOTILLA 13

FLOTILLA 13

Israeli Naval Commandos in the Red Sea, 1967–1973

Rear Admiral Ze'ev Almog

NAVAL INSTITUTE PRESS
Annapolis, Maryland

Naval Institute Press
291 Wood Road
Annapolis, MD 21402

Library of Congress Cataloging-in-Publication Data
Almog, Ze'ev, 1935–
  ['Atalefim ba-Yam ha-adom. English]
  Flotilla 13 : Israeli commandos in the Red Sea, 1967–1973 / Ze'ev Almog.
      p. cm.
  Includes bibliographical references and index.
  ISBN 978-1-59114-015-3
  1. Israel. Hel-ha-yam—Commando troops. 2. Israel-Arab War, 1973. 3. Naval
tactics. 4. Commando troops. 5. Israel—History, Naval. I. Title.
  DS128.14.H45A4613 2010
  359.9'84—dc22

                                                         2010022122

Printed in the United States of America on acid-free paper.

14 13 12 11 10   9 8 7 6 5 4 3 2
First printing

Contents

Acknowledgments

The publication of this book would not have been possible without the support and help of many dear friends and colleagues.

I wrote this book in memory of Flotilla 13th's warriors who lost their lives in combat operations that I commanded and are described in this book: Dani Levi, Haim Shturman, Yoav Shahar, Oded Nir, Rafi Miloh, and Shlomo Eshel. I shall always cherish their memory.

I also wrote this book in honor and admiration for an exceptional group of people, soldiers, and officers who served with me in the Israeli Naval Commando Unit, and took part in difficult operations under my command and the command of others. This small group of people put Flotilla 13 at the forefront of the Israeli Navy and military operations and wrote a remarkable chapter in their history book.

I am deeply indebted to two commanders and friends who have mentored and supported me for more than half a century: Captain Itzhak Rahav ("Izzi"), who was the commander of Flotilla 13 when I joined it and encouraged me to volunteer to serve in the unit and in the Israeli Navy; and General Israel Tal ("Talik"), Deputy Chief of Staff of the Israeli Defense Forces during the 1973 war who has inspired me with his wisdom and leadership.

Throughout my career I had the privilege and honor of working with remarkable Americans who provided great support to me, the Israel Navy, and to the State of Israel: Admiral Thomas Hayward, a former CNO of the U.S. Navy, with whom I had the privilege of serving when I was the C.I.C. of the Israeli Navy. Since that time our friendship has only become stronger. The late Captain Ted Fielding, commander of the U.S. Navy SEALs, and the late Rear Admiral Chuck Le-Moyne with whom I trained and became friends; and my dear friend Lee Mansi, Lieutenant Commander U.S. Navy (Res.), also a U.S. Navy SEAL officer, and a true American hero. My friends Rear Admiral George Worthington and Rear Admiral Cathal ("Irish") Flynn, who have enlightened me with their ideas about naval special operations. My dear friend Captain Abe Greenberg, U.S. Navy (Ret.), another American hero, who was my sponsor at the Naval War College. Abe has reviewed this book and has contributed immensely to its publication. I shall always be indebted to him.

The book was published originally in Hebrew by the Israeli Defense Ministry and the Galili Center for Defense Studies at the initiative of Lieutenant Colonel (Ret.) Avraham Zohar and Shlomo Sela. I thank them.

Finally, I am deeply grateful to my wife, Dr. Geula Almog, for her continuous support, love, constructive suggestions, and enlightening comments.

Ze'ev Almog

Note: Editing: Aryeh Idan (Hebrew version); translation (from Hebrew to English): Avi Aronsky; design and arrangement of diagrams and illustrations: Eliyahu Schwartz ("Metukah") and Dganit Kochli; design of maps on pp. 4, 137, and 139: Avigdor Orgad

Introduction

This book constitutes a refinement of the lectures I delivered in 2004–5 on the operations of the Shayetet (Flotilla) 13 (S-13)[1] during the War of Attrition and Yom Kippur War, within the framework of the seminar named "Special Operations in the Wars of Israel from 1943 to 1981." The seminar was sponsored by the Galili Center for Defense Studies, under the stewardship of Lieutenant Colonel (Res.) Avraham Zohar from the Association of Military History at Tel-Aviv University.

The work is the fruit of an in-depth study of the large array of relevant historical material on the topic at hand. In both my oral and written presentation, I leaned on the following sources: the authorized sources of the Israeli Defense Forces (IDF); historical research and scholarly publications on the War of Attrition, such as the research conducted by the above-mentioned Avraham Zohar and Dr. Mustafa Kabha of Tel-Aviv University; my personal acquaintance with the figures involved; and the knowledge that I accumulated throughout my thirty-three years of service in the IDF, which included five of Israel's wars. I took an active part in all these wars, and some of the campaigns that were waged in between, as either a combat soldier or officer. Over the course of my tenure in the Israeli Navy—both within and outside of the S-13—I gained experience in all the combat and command levels of naval commando operations. During the period in which I commanded the S-13, which encompassed the War of Attrition, there was a dramatic increase in its operational activity. Accordingly, the units' combat force was built up and ultimately doubled; its combat methods were consolidated; and new combat and organizational means were forged.

The first part of the book chronicles my tenure as the commander of the S-13, from May 1968 to October 1971. I recount my efforts to overcome the S-13's trauma from the Six Day War and get it back in the saddle again by carrying out special operations in the marine theater. My objective was to rehabilitate the organization that I was reared in, and whose commandos and staff I loved, and thus help the S-13 reclaim its standing as an active combat unit.

I am well aware of the "danger of subjectivity" that hovers over my doorstep. That said, my rendition of the facts and assessment of the unit's achievements are primarily based on the ample store of authorized sources and the testimony of officers and combat soldiers that personally took part in all the relevant events. Moreover, the lectures were given before an audience with a genuine interest in this topic—among them, senior members of the Navy and other IDF corps—and elicited insightful responses, many of which completed or elucidated my thoughts. Some of these remarks have been duly incorporated into the chapters of this book. Consequently, I believe that I have managed to complement, at least partially, the personal vantage point that informs my account with the research and perspective of others.

A special operation is one that is conducted behind enemy lines by a relatively small force with limited means for the purpose of attaining a broad military and political objective. The central defining element of a special operation is the surprise factor. In a naval commando operation, the troops endeavor to catch the enemy off guard by taking advantage of a sea route.

The Israeli Navy Commando's special operations date back to the missions that were carried out by naval squadrons under the purview of the *Palmach's*[2] Marine Demolition Unit, even before the establishment of the State of Israel in 1948. In the War of Independence, this unit was succeeded by the S-13, which sank the *Emir Farouk*, the flagship of the Egyptian navy.

From the end of the War of Independence until the Six Day War, the S-13 —or for that matter the entire Navy—did not conduct any combat operations on enemy territory. The Shayetet's lone attempt to conduct an independent fighting action throughout this period was on March 16, 1962, when the S-13 was slated to attack the Kursi Outpost within the framework of Operation Snunit (swallow), the Golani Brigade's retaliatory raid against Syrian positions along the shores of the Sea of Galilee. However, the S-13's troops were ordered to return before they managed to step foot on enemy shore.

During the Six Day War, five naval task forces, including units from the S-13, attacked Egypt's and Syria's major ports and their points of ingress, but returned without having accomplished their missions. At a conference of senior navy officers some eight months after the war, Chief of the General Staff Haim Bar-Lev still felt the need to castigate the Shayetet for its subpar performance.

In the half year that followed the outbreak of the Six Day War, the Navy was stricken by three enormous tragedies: its erroneous attack on the *Liberty*, an American intelligence ship; the sinking of the INS *Eilat* by Egyptian forces; and the disappearance of the INS *Dakar*, a submarine. This, then, was the reality I was asked to contend with upon being appointed to command the S-13 on May 8, 1968.

The S-13 carried out numerous special operations over the course of the War of Attrition, and the ensuing Yom Kippur War, which broke out in 1969 and 1973, respectively. During that period, the scope, frequency, complexity, and quality of these operations steadily grew in what for the Shayetet was a historically unprecedented fashion. What's more, many of the Shayetet's special operations during the War of Attrition and the Yom Kippur War constituted a paradigm for subsequent maritime special operations, such as the naval antiterrorist operations and seizure of a beachhead during Operation Peace of the Galilee in 1982.

The first chapter of this book focuses on the state of affairs and infrastructure that formed the backdrop for the consolidation of new and unique Israeli patterns of operation in the marine theater and the construction of central prototypes for the Navy Commando's special operations. Both the second and third chapters are devoted to operations during the War of Attrition: the second chapter depicts and analyzes the amphibious assault against the fortress on Green Island, and the third chapter surveys Operation Escort, in which two Egyptian torpedo boats were sunk in the Gulf of Suez. The fourth chapter examines the four raids on the Hurgada Anchorage in the north of the Red Sea during the Yom Kippur War.

FLOTILLA
13

ONE

Navy Commando
in the War of Attrition

Introduction

On account of the Navy's failures during the Six Day War and the year that followed, a "psychological barrier" took form both within and outside the ranks of the Shayetet 13 (S-13), which prevented the unit from returning to operational activity. A qualitative transformation, or what organizational psychologists refer to as a "second-order change," was needed to rehabilitate the unit. Although every reform naturally triggers objections, in the case of the S-13 the doubters managed to erect a steep wall of difficulties, which would have to be surmounted in order to engender the requisite change.

At the outset of my tenure as the S-13's commander, I was convinced that the key to the unit's effort to turn the corner and fully recover was an operational mission that would be executed according to the book and meet the IDF's expectations. However, I was faced with a litany of problems and questions:

- How would we find a combat mission that would enable the unit to get over the hump?
- Once a suitable operation was found, how would we convince the IDF's General Staff, which had its doubts concerning the soldiers' professional and psychological state of readiness, that the S-13 was indeed capable of fulfilling the mission?

- After blowing a huge opportunity during the Six Day War, how would the Navy's admirals win back the senior brass' confidence in its ability to command combat operations?

- Due to the shortcomings during the Six Day War and the ensuing year, the Navy command had assumed a critical attitude toward the S-13, and there were serious reservations about entrusting it to carry out combat missions. Under the circumstances, what could be done to tip the scales back in our favor?

- The S-13 was undermanned. Its entire combat force consisted of only thirty-two commandos and training new operators would take a considerable amount of time. How would we maximize the scarcity in manpower and correspondingly double our manpower?

- Many of the soldiers that remained in the Shayetet after the war were bitter and high-strung. How would we bolster their morale and self-image?

- There were fears that the sub-par state of the unit's munitions would let us down. How would we convince the powers that be to outfit the unit with new weapons in an environment of mistrust?

The Geo-Strategic Status Quo in the Aftermath of the Six Day War

The ramifications of the Six Day War provided the S-13 with an opportunity to return to the operational stage. The addition of some 500 miles of coastline to Israel's borders had spawned a new geo-political reality in which the majority of territory under its control was surrounded by water. This change also engendered a new military reality, for any ground operation on enemy territory would necessitate the traversal of a water obstacle.

Within two years of Israel's stunning victory in the Six Day War, troops along both sides of the Israeli-Egyptian divide engaged in a bloody slugfest—an undeclared state of belligerency known as the War of Attrition. One school of thought assumes that the War of Attrition lasted for three entire years. This camp bases its argument on the time period that President Gamal Abdel Nasser of Egypt allocated to General Muhammad Fawzi, the commander of the Egyptian armed forces, on June 11, 1967, for rehabilitating the army. In addition, Nasser ordered Fawzi to inflict five Israeli casualties per day during that same time period.[1] According to the adherents of this theory, the War of Attrition commenced on the tails of the Six Day War and ended some three years later, with the signing of the United States and Soviet Union–mediated cease-fire agreement between Israel and Egypt on August 8, 1970.

Alternatively, there are those who claim that the War of Attrition was waged from March 1969 to August 1970. This estimate corresponds with the intensity of the incidents and the number of losses,[2] as well as to what Nasser himself termed *kharb al-istinizaf*—the bloodletting war, or what *Aman* (the IDF's Directorate of Military Intelligence) translated as "attrition"—in his speech on July 23, 1969 (following the S-13's assault on Green Island and the Israeli Air Force's first massive bombardment along the length of the Suez Canal, Operation Boxer). In contrast, the subsequent "liberation" phase, as Nasser put it, was intended to be a full-fledged, multi-front war against Israel. It is worth noting that King Husayn of Jordan, the Palestinians, and the rest of Israel's "eastern front" had reached an understanding with Nasser whereby they agreed to give the Egyptian army all the time it needed to prepare for the "liberation" stage, which they too were destined to take part in.[3]

The War of Attrition—Implications and Plans

On March 10, 1968, Nasser delivered a speech before Egyptian soldiers stationed on the canal front, which was of utmost importance to the S-13, for it outlined the four stages of his war plan: "We are now laboring, and will continue to labor, until we pass from the *sumud* [firm stand] phase to the *dafaa waqaai* [preventive defense] phase, from which we will proceed to *al-rade* [the deterrence] phase, and then to the *tahrir* [liberation] phase and the final victory."[4] If Nasser would indeed abide by his stated schedule, the S-13 would have enough time, until the "liberation phase," to methodically implement its own reconstruction plan. From a geo-strategic standpoint, the War of Attrition thus constituted an appropriate context for the recovery and rise of the S-13.

The Shayetet's recovery plan was predicated on several components. During the first phase of the plan, the intention was to concentrate the majority of its operational activity on joint enterprises with the Sayeret Matkal (an elite special operations unit officially referred to as Unit 269). It was hoped that the modest collaboration between the two commando units would gradually expand, merit the recognition of the top brass, and develop into independent and targeted operations.

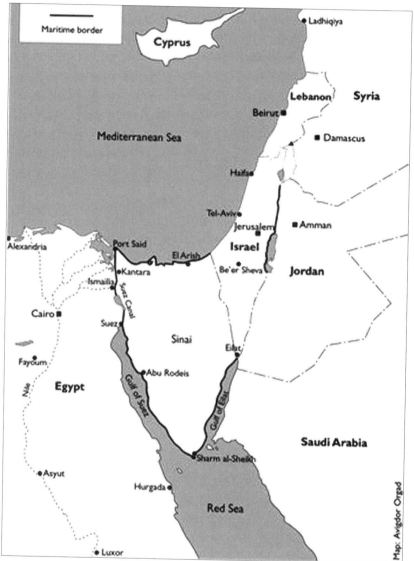

Maritime borders and water obstacles in the aftermath of the Six Day War.

The S-13's joint activities with the Sayeret were conducted along the Suez Canal. The significance and practical utility of these operations were as follows:

■ Given the physical layout of the canal, we were able to base our initial activities entirely on swimming, diving, and kayaking. This enabled us to reach the target without motor vessels, which had yet to reach the requisite level of dependability.

- The troops were taught rudimentary standing operating procedure (SOP) methods. Moreover, they adopted and fine-tuned combat norms, such as adhering to the mission, military professionalism, and discipline.

In sum, the cooperation and tight relations with the Sayeret Matkal's commandos and officers were intended to help the Shayetet's soldiers master the new operational approach and carry out the missions that were expected of them.

The second phase entailed leveraging the operational activity as a springboard for accumulating experience and improving the soldiers' infantry skills. As noted above, the change in the contours of Israel's borders necessitated the traversal of water barriers. I assumed that the operational integration of infantry combat in the Shayetet's training program was a key to enhancing the unit's reputation in the eyes of the senior brass. Although infantry drills were already included in the S-13's commando training route, it was hitherto only a training device that was not translated into or directed toward actual combat experience (save for those troops that happened to participate in fighting during their combat training outside of the S-13's purview). The S-13 did not introduce an in-house framework for teaching infantry combat and implementing it on the battlefield until 1968.

By dint of my personal acquaintance with the Sayeret Matkal's commander, Lieutenant Colonel Uzi Yairi, an unofficial pact was struck between the commando units. According to the agreement, the Sayeret's training officer (Captain Yossi Kaplan) would train our commandos in the art of infantry combat, and the S-13's officers would teach the Sayeret's soldiers marine skills (e.g., swimming, moving in and operating rubber crafts, and traversing water barriers). As a result of this collaboration, the S-13's commandos mastered a wide array of infantry combat skills, while polishing up on the methods, means, and techniques that are required for surmounting a water obstacle and infiltrating enemy territory. In addition, a close working relationship was forged between the two units.

During the third phase of the S-13's rehabilitation program, the unit regularly supported IDF operations that involved crossing the Jordan River and the

Dead Sea. The brunt of the activity in this sector—whose defense perimeter was more dispersed than the Egyptian front—was on land, so that the missions in these zones of operation were relatively simple. The 1968–69 Routine Security Measures Report indeed indicates that "the majority of the Navy's assistance to IDF forces in ground operations revolved around the activities . . . of Unit 707 and the S-13, within the framework of the 'Girit' [badger] Operations that necessitated the traversal of the Jordan River to and from targets. . . . In Operation Tshurah (the attack on Beirut's airport in December 1968), the Navy was on alert off the beach of the zone of action."[5]

Although the opportunity for displaying the full range of the Shayetet's unique virtues were rather limited in these theaters, I reasoned that it was incumbent upon the S-13 to contribute wherever possible, regardless of the terrain or complexity of the mission. It was important for us to earn a reputation as a force that is not picky. In other words, the S-13 would endeavor to be readily available and highly professional at all times.

The fourth phase was a concerted effort to provide comprehensive training to the S-13's officers and soldiers and to improve the methods, combat means, and SOP of the entire unit (to include combat support personnel). All these activities were directed toward improving our combat readiness. Consequently, the training was specifically suited to the sectors that we operated in as well as the particular needs and combat policy of the IDF.

The S-13's general recovery program was grounded on six central pillars. The first pillar called for an in-depth study and analysis of the Navy's failures during the Six Day War, with an emphasis on the education of junior-ranking officers and the graduates of the operators' course. My underlying premise was that unless the S-13 recognized the importance of learning from past mistakes in an unvarnished manner, we would condemn ourselves to repeating them. The stress was thus placed on evaluating the conditions and processes that were responsible for the S-13's unsuccessful operations. The historical research indicates that the unit's poor showing in 1967–68 primarily stemmed from a failure to adhere to the mission, a lack of military professionalism and discipline, and negligent preparation and management of the missions on the part of all the command levels.

The second pillar consisted of revising the commando training route. From that point on, all the facets of infantry training were concentrated at the beginning of the track, during basic training, the company commander course, and the parachuting course. Thereafter, all the specialist courses were given in succession: introductory marine, basic combat diving, and lastly an advanced tactical course. This reform was designed to provide a long-range solution for the unit's operational needs, whose results would only be seen at the end of the training route a year and a half later. In addition, it was intended to improve the culling and placement of volunteers at the outset of the selection process and to ratchet up the number of candidates that were ultimately accepted into the S-13.

The third pillar entailed a redistribution of all the tasks that were assigned to the S-13's various members and combat units. From that point on, all the combat soldiers were qualified as both divers and ground raiders! The objective behind this reform was to create a versatile soldier, so that the tasks and exertions required of each commando would be distributed equally among all the combat units: explosive/mother boats and the "pigs" (tiny submarines), which run on electric power and are similar to the Italian-made *maiale*), "foot" divers (combat divers who advance themselves without a motorized vehicle), and the instructors in the S-13 school. Since it also helped solve our shortage in combat manpower, this reform was executed at once. The even distribution of diving and infiltration responsibilities among all the combat units gave rise to several marked improvements:

- On the one hand, it created a high standard according to which every soldier was capable of contending with a high threshold of exertion and dangerous assignments. On the other hand, it conferred a sense of equality between each of the S-13's combat units in all that concerned team pride and morale.

- It produced a large reservoir of combat divers and marine raiders. As a result, we were able to extract the maximum out of the limited number of soldiers that were in the Shayetet at the time. (In fact, it was only thanks to this reform that the S-13 had enough commandos to carry out the assault on Green Island.)

- The apportioning of assignments between the S-13's divers (as per the level of difficulty) and raiders (in accordance with the volume of their particular occupations) enabled the soldiers from the other combat units to devote enough time to exercises that pertained to their specific professions. Consequently, every soldier was at full battle readiness in his particular field of expertise.

The fourth pillar was the development of new combat techniques and methods that immeasurably improved the S-13's operational capacity, especially the unit's surreptitious entry and navigational skills:

- From that point on, webbing gear and weapons were the only equipment that commandos would take ashore. Moreover, the days of landing on shore with boats were over, as the exclusive means for reaching the enemy shore would be via swimming or diving. The purpose of these measures was to ensure stealthy entry and circumvent obstacles that stemmed from the features of the shoreline, the sea state, or difficulties that pertained to docking the crafts or removing them from the beach.
- The pig, which operates above the surface of the water, at surface level ("minimal buoyancy"), and underneath the sea, was hitherto manned by only two soldiers. However, two more soldiers were added to the crew in order to improve the S-13's surreptitious entries. The additional men could assume infantry combat roles and/or carry loads and weapons. This enabled the S-13 to increase its loads and transport them over considerable distances (about fifty miles back and forth), unlike the foot diver who is incapable of bearing similar cargos due to the weight or distance involved.
- The S-13 started to avail itself of one of the Air Force's electronic guidance systems. When conventional navigation methods proved too difficult or uncertain, the device would help direct the unit's crafts to the designated positions in enemy territory.

Notwithstanding the shortage of weapons at our disposal and the antiquated and unreliable, if not dangerous, condition of those in stock, the fifth pillar called for improving the dependability of our existing weapons. My working assumption was that the S-13 would only be able to acquire new and more sophisticated weapons once it had proven its operational prowess. As a result, the S-13 took the following measures:

- The operators continued to get around in Mark III inflatable crafts, but their capacity was limited to four soldiers who could only take along their personal arms and a scuba set. Heavier cargos caused the engines to overheat and shudder, which tended to slow the boat down, if not debilitate it altogether. These glitches naturally placed the soldiers at risk, disrupted missions, and even caused some missions to be scrubbed or aborted.

- We shored up two Mark V inflatable boats, which were pilfered from the Sayeret Matkal (incidentally, the Sayeret also acquired them via "unconventional" means). The maximum capacity was set at six soldiers per boat. Moreover, changes and adjustments were introduced that rendered the Mark Vs operational and seaworthy.

- Weapons, ammunition, charges, personal communication devices, and other equipment were insulated against water pressure at the S-13's workshops. As a result, the Shayetet's operators were basically the only IDF soldiers capable of executing ground-based infantry operations after swimming and diving to the zone of operation.

- We devised an integrated combat webbing gear that was suitable for both diving and infantry tasks. The model was developed in the early 1960s, but for some reason they didn't continue to manufacture the webbing gear for all the commandos.

The sixth pillar called for adapting the techno-logistical system to the conditions in the Sinai Theater. The road from the S-13's home base in Atlit (on the site of an old crusader fortress near Haifa) to the northern tip of the Suez Canal was about 370 miles long. What's more, the road was teeming with physical obstacles—potholes, ditches, and roadblocks—and operational dangers. For instance, the vehicles had to pass through the Gaza Strip and other regions that were susceptible to shelling, ambushes, and mines. The road fatigue and the danger of incurring casualties or exposing the aim of the mission along the way demanded a complete organizational and techno-logistical housecleaning as well as the development of appropriate methods and equipment—secured and concealed—for shuttling troops and equipment and landing the S-13's principal pieces (rubber crafts, mother boats, and pigs) at any point along the beaches of the northern Sinai or the Gulf of Suez, to include sites that lacked a defended pier or anchorage. To ensure that weapons and support equipment reached the combat zone in a timely fashion and in working order, the entire transport process had to be capable of working under a tight schedule. The factors that impeded the rapid and secure transfer of equipment, and thus demanded a solution, were as follows:

- In accordance with SOP, several senior officers had to give their approval before the S-13 could embark on any mission. If, for example, the operation was in conjunction with the Sayeret, it required the clearance of no less than four commanders: the admiral of the Navy, the commander of the Southern Command, the commander of armored forces in Sinai, and the chief of the Directorate of Military Intelligence (*Aman*). Alternatively, an infantry operation occasionally needed the consent of the chief commander of the Paratroopers and the Infantry Corps (*Katzchar*), the head of the Operations Directorate (*Agam*), and of course the IDF commander in chief. In other words, the S-13 was forced to contend with a long and complicated command pipeline that did not always suit our frequently tight schedules.

- In the past, operators would prepare most of their vessels and combat kits on their own. This took up valuable time, which could have been devoted to operational matters. Henceforth, techno-logistical echelons ("the forward team") would tend to *all* the pieces and weapons, with the exception of personnel combat equipment, such as scuba sets, personal arms, and ammunition, which would be handled by the operators themselves. This new arrangement necessitated a clear division of responsibilities and new forming-up regulations. With this in mind, new criteria were established for sorting out and classifying the preparatory steps for an operation, whereby tasks were assigned to either the technical or combat echelons based on the nature of the equipment and pieces. This was an unprecedented organizational measure whose efficaciousness was twofold: it freed up time for the operators who were thus able to devote the majority of the SOP period to briefings, studying intelligence, and meticulously preparing for the mission; and the supporting echelon prepared the pieces on their own in a professional, exacting, and responsible manner. In consequence, the quality of both echelons' preparations during SOP improved beyond compare.

- Hitherto, only combat soldiers reported to the staging grounds. As a result, they did not have the requisite logistical and technical support at their immediate disposal. Under the new deployment regulations, the S-13's top experts in all the pertinent techno-logistical fields (engines, electricity, communications, electronics, devices, rubbery, field cookery, bivouacking, and more) accompanied the combat troops down to the assembly points in Sinai. The support units were thus able to provide a swift, optimal response to any professional or logistical problem that arose in the field until the very moment before final departure.

During this period, the Canal Zone was the IDF's principal front, and I believed that the area would expand toward its flanks, especially in the direction of the northern Gulf of Suez. The region contained important strategic targets and military installations, which were arrayed within a relatively small territory, along the coast and in the heart of the sea. I assumed that dependable pigs and trained commandos could reach, penetrate, and inflict damage on these targets, or at the very least offer palpable assistance in an attack. What's more, in my estimation, the S-13 operators stood to become the "tip of the IDF's sword" on the Egyptian front, particularly in the area of the Red Sea to the south of the Canal. Consequently, we were preoccupied with qualifying the pigs from an operational and techno-logistical standpoint, with an emphasis on the following topics:

- Training divers who were to be added to the standard crew of two pig operators.
- We constructed what was dubbed the "rocking cradle" for the pig. This was essentially a platform with steel springs at its base, which cushioned the mounted pig from the convulsions along the pothole-filled route. The cradle thereby ensured that these vital crafts would reach the theater of action in one piece.
- We developed secure and concealed land transport mechanisms for the pig. The latter was stored (along with the "cradle") in a closed container along with all the other necessary support equipment (accumulators, electric chargers, compressors, etc.), so that the container constituted a hidden workshop for lowering the pig into the sea. The entire container was loaded as a single unit onto a closed and covered semitrailer, which was driven or shipped off (at times via Eilat) to the theater of action in Sinai.
- Means were also needed for lowering the pig into the water at any point along the coast. With this in mind, we converted a "Rio" truck crane,

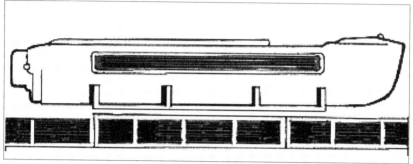

A "pig" on a "rocking cradle."

which was already in the service of the armed corps, into a tool for transporting the pig from the road to the shore and hoisting it over the water,
before dropping the vessel into the sea.

The Navy Commando in the War of Attrition

Following the spring of 1968, the Shayetet was in the midst of a gradual over-
haul, namely a systematic increase in the size, complexity, and frequency of its
operational activities, in which the unit's commandos were also honing their
professional skills. All these changes took into account the geostrategic situation in the various theaters of operation in an effort to provide an appropriate
response to the army's policies and needs, so that the S-13's above-mentioned
reforms conformed to the general guidelines and deployments of the IDF.
Overall, this period of significant progress can be divided into six phases.

THE FIRST PHASE: INDEPENDENT TRAVERSAL OF WATER BARRIERS
The initial phase of the S-13's transformation consisted of the following
missions:

- Operation Asuta (April 1968). Two officers from the S-13 (myself included) slipped across enemy territory and advanced to the opening of the
  tunnel on the Yarmouk River, along the Israeli-Jordanian-Syrian border.
  The mission was to examine the possibility of flooding the Ghor Canal by
  blowing up the doors of the tunnel. In light of our findings, it was decided
  not to go ahead with the demolition operation.

- Operation Pier Outpost, Port Tawfiq (May 1968). Four commandos and the Shayetet's commander planted four barrels of dynamite into the seabed at the entrance to the Suez Canal. As a result, the IDF had the option of sinking Egyptian boats by setting off the explosives from the adjacent Pier Outpost.

- Operation Boger (May 1968). Six kayakers infiltrated the pools to the east of Port Fuad, north of the canal, and mined the dirt embankments around the edge of one of the pools, which served as an embarkation point for Egyptian intelligence missions. The charges subsequently went off on an Egyptian patrol. Similar surreptitious entries were also executed along the eastern coast of the Dead Sea.

THE SECOND PHASE: COLLABORATION WITH THE SAYERET AND SUPPORT OF WATER CROSSINGS

This phase encompassed a series of recon patrols that were collectively referred to as the Penguin Operations, which were carried out on all the dark nights of 1968. The S-13 helped the Sayeret Matkal cross the Suez Canal for the purpose of gathering intelligence behind Egyptian lines. Our job was to secure a beachhead, safeguard it, and transport the Sayeret's troops to and from the opposite bank.

Following the Penguin Operations, Haim Bar-Lev, the chief of the General Staff, wrote the following letter to the Shayetet's commander on December 2, 1968:

LTCD Ze'ev Almog
Commander of the Shayetet 13
[c.c.] Admiral of the Navy
Subject: Operation Penguin—Commendation
The flawless execution of Operation Penguin has once again proven that there is no limit to the operational ability, improvisational skill, and above all the dedication and valor of spirit of the Israeli diver.

I hereby commend you, Ze'ev, and through you all the Shayetet's people who took part in the enterprise for your devoted labor and impressive accomplishment.

Haim Bar-Lev—Lieutenant General
Chief of the General Staff

As a result of these missions, the S-13's reputation as a capable force began to grow roots and yield fruit. The confirmation of the unit's wherewithal was subsequently manifested in the multifaceted and independent operations that we were entrusted with, even if their scope was still rather small.

There was no change in the status quo along the Suez Canal between April 1968 and April 1969 (the IDF's work year). Following the Six Day War, the canal was closed to all merchant shipping and international shipping. Moreover, the seaway formed a dividing line between the Egyptian and Israeli armies, which were arrayed against each other along its banks. Although the Egyptian army managed to reorganize itself with the help of Soviet military experts and arms, it still lacked the confidence to dare cross the canal. As in the previous year, the only engagements between Israeli and Egyptian forces were occasional shooting incidents and minor combat operations.

Throughout this period, the Egyptians were usually the belligerents, and they indeed managed to inflict some heavy damage upon the IDF. For example, twenty-five Israeli troops were killed and another fifty-six were wounded during an upsurge in violence between September and October 1968. Most of these losses were due to the weakness of the Israeli fortification lines, which enabled the Egyptian army to catch the IDF off guard by means of effective artillery fire against its frontline and rear forces. Another escalation in Egyptian attacks was effected toward the end of this period, from January to April 1969.

The IDF refused to resign itself to a defensive posture. Heavy Egyptian shelling along the Canal Zone between September and October 1968 led to Operation Helem (shock) on October 31. The Israeli riposte consisted of demolition operations against three targets deep within Egypt: Kanah Bridge and Hammadi Dam-Bridge, both on the Nile, and the transformer station southeast of Nag Hammadi. The bridges and the dam were hit with hollow charges, which were thrown from IDF helicopters, while the transformer station was hit by an airborne force of the 35th (Paratrooper) Brigade, under the command of Captain Matan Vilnai. Besides killing two enemy sentries and destroying a car, the assault on the station caused a blackout in Upper Egypt. These attacks on key infrastructure came as a shock to the Republican regime. Nasser abruptly suspended all the Egyptian combat initiatives along the canal and established a new guard, the People's Army, to defend the country's rear and its essential installations. Consequently, the IDF earned a respite of over four months, which it took advantage of to improve its defenses in western Sinai.

Egypt's accomplishments from September to October 1968 also precipitated a feverish effort on the part of the IDF to buttress its fortifications, primarily within the framework of Operation Maoz (stronghold). In late October, the Sinai Peninsula, including the Israeli bank of the canal, was reinforced with an additional armored brigade. The latter was subsequently integrated into a regular division,[6] which was established soon after under the command of Brigadier General Avraham Adan ("Bren"). Once the lion's share of Operation Maoz was completed in March 1969 and most of the fortifications contained projectile blocking layers, the IDF took the initiative. All told, the IDF inflicted heavier damage on the Egyptians in 1969 than in either 1967 or 1968.

THE THIRD PHASE: JOINT OPERATIONS—INDEPENDENT INFANTRY, RECONNAISSANCE, AND MARITIME DEMOLITION

The new politico-strategic status quo on the canal front paved the way for the next step in the S-13's professional progress: independent operations on enemy territory. This stage entailed joint infantry missions with other units, maritime demolition operations, and clandestine[7] surveys of enemy targets.

The third phase encompassed the following operations:

- Operation Lahav (blade) 30 (January 29, 1969). S-13 operators crossed the northern part of the Gulf of Suez on Mark V rubber crafts and laid a mine on the axis of the road along the Egyptian coast. Recently developed by the Engineer Corps, the roadside bomb was designed to be activated by the air pressure that is generated by a passing vehicle. However, the device went off prematurely, apparently due to the strong winds that prevail in this region, but none of the soldiers was injured.

- Bustan (orchard) (March 1969). Darting through the sea on a pig, three Shayetet operators conducted a clandestine survey of a "fuel island" located in the northwestern Gulf of Suez. Tankers weighing as much as 60,000 deadweight tons (dwt) delivered fuel to a terminal on the island, which then pumped the intake to refineries in the area. The mission's objective was to collect data for a plan to destroy the installation.

- Bustan 2 (March 13, 1969). Four operators reached the fuel island on board two pigs, whereupon they submerged and planted eight large mines on eight of the installation's fifteen support pillars (the Shayetet did not have additional charges at its disposal). The explosives were set off in one fell swoop, but the terminal remained on its feet. However, the blast apparently managed to undermine the structure; later on, an IDF tank shelled a tanker while it was linked up to the terminal, and the sunken vessel dragged down the entire installation to the seabed.

- The Morgan Oil field (early April 1969). Four operators on board two pigs—transported on the deck of the INS *Bat-Yam* auxiliary ship—reconnoitered the production platform of the Morgan Oil field, which is located in the heart of the Gulf of Suez, across from the town of Abu Rudeis. The intelligence was used to prepare a demolition operation, in the event that the IDF would decide to attack the installation. Despite rough seas, the mission was a success.

- Lahav 32 (April 20, 1969). A pair of pigs carrying eight divers headed out on a clandestine operation to survey the Green Island Fortress, the target of a possible IDF assault. Although the divers discovered that security was tight, they also managed to locate an infiltration point on the north side of the compound. In addition, they discovered that the water was deep enough at high tide for a covert entry and that there were no currents around the fortress at the designated hour of attack. Data was also collected on auxiliary sites and the movement of vessels in the vicinity.

During this phase, a new wrinkle was added to the Shayetet's collaboration with the Sayeret Matkal: the former helped the Sayeret traverse water obstacles and conduct infantry operations, such as ambushes along the canal line, which were headed by the Sayeret.

- Bulmus (ravenous hunger) 3 (May 10, 1969). Fifteen commandos from the Sayeret Matkal, led by Lieutenant Colonel Menachem Digli (who replaced Uzi Yairi as the unit's commander), set up a roadside ambush to the west of the sweet water canal in the northern part of the Suez Canal. The canal was traversed with the help of three Mark I rubber crafts. Upon reaching the Egyptian bank, an S-13 force, comprised of eight operators,

seized a beachhead and secured the crossing point. A patrol fell into the ambush; the Sayeret force killed two enemy soldiers and destroyed their vehicle, while all the IDF troops returned safely.

- Bulmus 4 (May 13, 1969). Another attempt was made to set up an ambush using the same approach and force alignment that had succeeded three days earlier. Right before embarkation, an Egyptian soldier was spotted near the targeted ambush site by an IDF observation post on the east bank. Consequently, the Sayeret Matkal decided to move the crossing point about a half mile to the south and proceed with the mission. I personally voiced my opposition on the grounds that the new location had yet to be properly reconnoitered and was too close to the previous ambush. Above all, I objected to crossing the canal on rubber vessels and preferred that the troops swim across, for there was a greater likelihood of boats being detected by the enemy. It is also worth noting that this particular crossing not only ran counter to my own personal opinion, but to the professional guidelines of the S-13. Despite my warnings, the mission proceeded as planned from the new site. A pair of Egyptian soldiers, who were manning a nearby post, opened fire on the boats from short range. An officer from the Sayeret (Second Lieutenant Haim Ben-Yonah) was killed, and the rest of the force was forced to beat a hasty retreat, swimming back to the Israeli side under heavy fire. The failure of the mission cast a shadow over the S-13's relations with the Sayeret, and the partnership between the two units veered off in a new direction.

As noted in Dr. Mustafa Kabha's *The War of Attrition from the Perspective of Egyptian Sources*, the Egyptian army continued its incessant harassment of Israeli positions along the Canal Zone:

On April 23, Egypt announced that they were abrogating the ceasefire agreement in a unilateral fashion. For its part, Israel responded with a second attack on the power station at Nag Hammadi. Likewise, Israel began to systematically shell the cities of the canal as a means for pressuring the Egyptians into ending the War of Attrition. But even the heavy damage that was inflicted on the economic infrastructure of the canal's cities, as well as the flight of the residents (some one million people) and the problems that were created due to the abandonment of houses and [the masses] streaming towards Cairo, did not persuade the Egyptians to cease taking the offensive.[8]

In response, the IDF unleashed a barrage of cannon fire, which triggered heavy artillery exchanges over the length of the Canal Zone. The General Staff also authorized the above-mentioned attack on the fuel island in March 1969 and the paratroopers' raids in the Nile Valley. On the night of April 29–30, 1969, paratroopers attacked an Egyptian high voltage power line, dam, and bridge (Operations Bustan and Batzoret). Yet none of these measures precipitated the coveted cease-fire, and the IDF gradually came to the realization that it could no longer relegate itself to these sorts of operation. The senior brass decided that the time had come to hammer enemy positions along the front line and its flanks. This decision led to the two aforementioned ambushes across the canal (Bulmus 3 and Bulmus 4), but these operations also failed to significantly alter the state of affairs. Consequently, operations officers at the General Staff, Southern Command, and Chief Infantry and Paratroops Officer Headquarters all scoured about for targets whose destruction would underscore the IDF's combat superiority, bolster Israel's power of deterrence, and persuade the Egyptians to silence their cannons.

This, then, formed the backdrop for the decision to seriously consider an assault against the defended compound on the Adabiyah peninsula.

THE FOURTH PHASE: INDEPENDENT INFANTRY RAIDS UNDER
THE SHAYETET'S COMMAND

Six days after the second Bulmus ambush, the Shayetet reconnoitered the coastal outpost on the Adabiyah peninsula in preparation for a possible raid against that target. This patrol set new standards and constituted another turning point in the Shayetet's standing, as it marked the culmination and confluence of two eventful decisions: on the macro level, the IDF intensified its operations against Egypt; and on the micro level, the senior brass authorized the S-13 to conduct independent amphibious assaults at platoon strength or greater. From the Shayetet's standpoint, this was no less than a "crossing of the Rubicon."

At the time, the Shayetet was at the height of preparations, exercises, and experiments that were aimed at consolidating its combat plan and techniques for the assault on Green Island. Correspondingly, the unit continued to lay ambushes with the Sayeret Matkal along the canal line. In light of the dearth in essential up-to-date intelligence on Adabiyah, the possibility arose of having the Shayetet clandestinely survey the targeted coast. Alongside the need for intelligence, I was admittedly spurred on by another motive. An argument—a taste of which I had already sampled in an earlier meeting with the chief infantry and paratroopers' officer—had surfaced over which unit was most fit to spearhead the actual raid. In my estimation, the successful conduct of the recon patrol would serve as a "down payment" for the keys to the mission itself.

Dwelling "at the shore of the sea," Adabiyah was a defended target that was built on a shoal and surrounded by swamps. The compound was equipped with detection and surveillance systems, and was supported by artillery fire and mobile forces on the coast and at sea. According to intelligence sources in *Aman*, the Egyptian units in the area were capable of responding to an alert and reaching the compound within approximately thirty minutes.

Even so, I was fully convinced that the Shayetet enjoyed a clear-cut advantage over the enemy: the ability to pounce straight out of the water and stealthily infiltrate any coastal site, regardless of the terrain or sea state. No less important was the fact that the S-13 could get to places that even the most elite ground forces would be hard-pressed to reach. For the better part of a year, the commandos had been practicing covert amphibious assaults onto the shore in both small and large groups, which swam or dove to the target from a point out at sea. By dint of a concerted effort, the S-13 had also improved its ground-based combat tactics. Consequently, I assumed that we would be able to surprise and pummel the enemy, a fact that I persistently drove home to the troops.

On May 19, 1969, a force of eight operators, including the author, embarked on a mission to reconnoiter the coast along the Adabiyah peninsula in the northwestern Gulf of Suez on board two pigs. Our objective was to complete the intelligence picture for a ground assault against a compound, which was classified as a "coastal" or "radar station." The force availed itself of one

Bird's-eye view of Adabiyah.

of the Air Force's electronic GPSs, which helped the pig operators navigate their way to the target.

I had already designed a principal plan for the Shayetet's raid, but I knew that the plan would have to accord with the intelligence that would be assembled on the patrol. The force located a potential infiltration point and collected information on the target's point of ingress, the shape of the coastline, the currents near the shore, the local seabed, and the conditions at high tide. In addition, we got a feel for the level of security and enemy activity around the target, both of which appeared to be standard.

The assembled data and the plan that we proposed ultimately persuaded Lieutenant General Bar-Lev to assign the mission to the S-13. Upon receiving the assignment, the Shayetet toiled away on the ground assault for an entire month. The element of surprise was deemed to be the key to the operation's success. With this in mind, the plan called for the troops to swim to the objective from a drop-off point in the middle of the sea. These characteristics would enable us to carry out the mission with a relatively small force of twenty-five commandos.

Officers heading to the final briefing before the assault on Adabiyah.

The Assault on Adabiyah—Bulmus 5 (June 21, 1969). Before the raid, the General Staff defined the mission in the following words: "The Navy will assault the radar station at Ras Adabiyah, with the objective of liquidating the enemy forces at the station and destroying [the installation]."

The target reportedly contained a radar station, five buildings, a high communications antenna, and thirty-two soldiers; however, *Aman's* intelligence concerning the existence of radar turned out to be false. Given the danger of intervention on the part of enemy forces in the vicinity—ground patrols, ships from the nearby naval port at the town of Adabiyah, and enemy artillery—the operation had to be executed in a prompt and robust manner.

Twenty Shayetet commandos, divided into four details, comprised the assault force. Moreover, another five commandos set up an ambush to the west of the target's entrance in order to prevent backup forces from joining the fray and the defenders from escaping. I commanded over the mission from one of the seven rubber crafts that transported the force and was accompanied by the chief infantry and paratroopers' officer, Brigadier General Rafael Eitan ("Raful"). The commandos left the rubber boats about a third of a mile from the beach and swam the rest of the way. The attack force breached the target without being detected and thus managed to catch the enemy completely by surprise. It assailed the defended outpost on the sandbank and killed most of the defenders. Meanwhile, the commandos laying in wait at the entrance cut down several Egyptian soldiers attempting to flee. In all, thirty Egyptian soldiers were killed and the antenna, generator, and a substantial portion of the buildings were destroyed, while our troops suffered only two minor injuries.

The operation at Adabiyah was the first of its kind in the annals of the entire IDF. Three days later, the commander in chief wrote the following letter of commendation:

Confidential

Personal

Office of the Chief of the General Staff

Confidential Letter—2240 24

8th of *Tamuz 5729*

June 24, 69

Commander of the Shayetet 13

Admiral of the Navy

Chief Infantry and Paratroopers' Officer

Subject: Operation Bulmus 5

Ze'ev,

The flawless execution of Bulmus 5 once again proved that there is no limit to the level of execution, planning skill, and above all the solemn devotion and spirit of valor of the Israeli diver.

Please pass on my highest esteem to the Shayetet commandos that took an active part in the operation, especially to LCDR Shaul Ziv, who commanded over the force that stormed [the position].

I am certain that my esteem for the commando is shared by the IDF and the entire nation.

Best wishes,

Haim Bar-Lev, Lieutenant-General

Chief of the General Staf

Dr. Kabha describes the repercussions of this operation on the Egyptians and the backdrop for the subsequent development of the S-13:

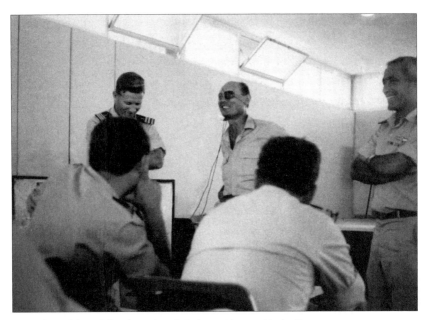

Debriefing of the Adabiyah raid, with Defense Minister Moshe Dayan.

From among its initiatives during that same period, the most prominent [Egyptian] operation was the attack on the tongue of Port Tawfiq. Israel used Fort Tawfiq as a base for shelling operations against Adabiyah and the ports of the Suez. The operation was conducted on the night of July 9, 1969. The Egyptian forces managed to hit three Israeli tanks. This operation was carried out by troops belonging to the III Army, which was established within the framework of the reconstruction of the armed forces. This was the [III] Army's maiden action. Egyptian commando forces again crossed the canal and attacked Israeli outposts. On June 30, 1969, Israel retaliated by bombarding the high voltage station near the city of Sohag. Even then, Moshe Dayan, the defense minister, warned that Israeli operations would not be limited to small-scale defensive counter actions, but are likely to be executed in a completely different way. The implementation of the decision began with the Israeli attack on a small Island in the Gulf of Suez, Green Island.[9]

The "different way" that Dayan was referring to was not late in coming. Soon thereafter, the IDF launched the assault on Green Island, which was followed on its heels by a massive bombardment along the canal on the part of the Israeli Air Force. Both operations were carried out for the intended purpose of deterring the Egyptians from initiating any further attacks.

THE FIFTH PHASE: GREEN ISLAND—A LARGE INFANTRY
RAID UNDER THE SHAYETET'S COMMAND

As noted above, the assault on Adabiyah constituted a turning point in the nature of the IDF's operations in Egypt, while the Green Island raid (July 20, 1969) signified the beginning of a second period in that same campaign, which would last until January 7, 1970. Bar-Lev's decision to transfer the assault on the Egyptian officers' club and medical corps' camp in the Great Bitter Lake from the Paratroopers to the Shayetet 13, and his subsequent acceptance of my proposal regarding Green Island were harbingers of the shift in the IDF's mind-set. Whereas the assault on the coastal station at Ras Adabiyah was indicative of the senior brass' de facto recognition of the Shayetet's ability to execute an extremely complicated ground assault against a built-up and defended land-based target, the assault on Green Island a mere month later constituted the de jure affirmation of our new standing.

The General Staff's decision to launch the assault on the Green Island Fortress came in the aftermath of a litany of losses along the Canal Zone. Egypt's campaign reached a crescendo on July 10 with a sunset raid against a tank depot on a pier to the south of Port Tawfiq, in which seven IDF soldiers were killed and five were wounded.

The S-13's raid against Green Island was preceded by an advance recon-naissance mission for another multi-dimensional operation: an IDF armored assault along the length of a wide strip of coast on the Gulf of Suez's west bank, which was scheduled for July 25. The recon patrol was conducted by a unit of defensive divers (Unit 707) on July 17, a mere two days before the Green Island raid, and the beach was found to be unfit for landing an armored force. Consequently, the operation was suspended indefinitely, at least until a more suitable location could be found.

Operation Bulmus 6 (July 19, 1969). Green Island is located in the upper reach-es of the Gulf of Suez, about a mile and a half southwest of Port Tawfiq. The island fortress was surrounded by walls that protruded straight out of the sea. About a hundred soldiers were stationed at the compound, which was fitted with a radar (that eventually turned out to be a phony) and emplacements equipped with medium and heavy machine guns, dual-purpose guns, and light cannons. There were other Egyptian forces—heavy artillery batteries, ships, and fighter jets—in the vicinity, which were capable of rushing over in the event of an IDF attack.

The prime objective of the Green Island assault was to strengthen the IDF's power of deterrence and force the Egyptians into suing for a cease-fire. The General Staff intentionally chose to wage a face-to-face battle in an ostensibly impenetrable target for the purpose of underscoring to the Egyptians the superiority of the Israeli combat soldier and to put to rest the notion that the IDF's prowess was entirely predicated on American technology.

The mission was jointly assigned to the S-13 and Sayeret Matkal, but the latter was placed under my command. The order that was issued was, "To liquidate the enemy force on Green Island and incapacitate structures and guns situated on the island."

All the compound's features pointed to an intense, hard-fought battle: the island's location in the heart of the sea ruled out the possibility that its defenders would be able to escape; its complex and crammed layout; the abundance of soldiers stationed there; and the advantageous positions and considerable means at the enemy's disposal. Notwithstanding the obstacles involved, the enemy was completely neutralized and the mission—as defined in the battle order—was fully accomplished. Six of the S-13's commandos received citations for their part in the battle. However, the IDF also incurred seventeen casualties, including six dead. (See the next chapter for a comprehensive account of the entire operation.)

In consequence of the assault, the Egyptians reinforced their positions in the Gulf of Suez with two torpedo boats, which began to patrol the line from Port Adabiyah to Ras Abu Daraj, via the oil terminal at Ras Sadat. Unless the two Egyptian torpedo boats were sunk, the IDF would not be able to go ahead with its plans to land armored forces in this sector, and the assault was thus pushed off to a later date. In sum, the raid against Green Island, along with the Air Force's ensuing operations, managed to bolster Israel's power of deterrence.

An easterly view of the Green Island Fortress.

THE SIXTH PHASE: CLASSIC MINOR-TACTICS MARINE WARFARE

Despite incurring casualties during the assault on Green Island, the Shayetet did not cease its operational activity. The very next day marked the beginning of a forty-five-day period in which the S-13 prepared for and conducted three unprecedented marine operations:

Raviv Katan (light rain, August 13, 1969). Two pigs carrying eight commandos set out to clandestinely survey a point along the Egyptian shore of the Gulf of Suez, west of Ras Sudr. The objective was to determine whether a certain strip of beach was fit to serve as a landing point for an armored force, and the area was indeed found to be suitable. Moreover, the commandos searched for an appropriate maritime debarkation point from which to launch a mission to sink the above-mentioned torpedo boats, which were stationed near Ras Sadat.

The recon mission served as a "live drill" for the S-13's patented approach to surreptitious entries. Once again, the pigs and their operators proved to be in top form, as the force managed to evade the detection of the Egyptian torpedo boats patrolling in the area and complete the mission.

As noted, the destruction of the torpedo boats constituted a precondition for the landing of the armored force. By dint of its capacity to covertly attach limpet mines with delay mechanisms to the bottom of the boats, the Shayetet was chosen for the job, instead of the Air Force. The IDF command also realized that the closer the sinking was to the landing, the greater the chances of success, and the demolition operation was thus scheduled for the night before the landing.

The General Staff subsequently decided to delay the armored assault until September 5. The postponement mounted serious obstacles in the Shayetet's path. In any event, the basic plan was for the S-13 to orchestrate three landings over the course of three nights, during which the armored force would be incrementally shuttled, under the cover of darkness, from their base in Sharm al-Sheikh to the loading and dispersion point at Ras Sudr. However, the new date fell on a particularly dark night, so that it would not be easy to locate the torpedo boats, which were difficult targets to begin with on account of their flat profiles. What's more, we did not know the exact anchorage sites of the two boats. Therefore, the Shayetet would embark upon what we referred to as a "violent patrol" (commonly known as a combat patrol), whereby if the torpedo boats were not located, or were found to be on the move (as was the case on the night of Raviv Katan), we would not be able to plant the charges.

Operation Escort (September 5, 1969). Notwithstanding the uncertain conditions, a squadron of "pigs" was ordered to proceed to the conjectured anchorage site and attempt to attach the limpet mines. The operators sighted the targets, but the two Egyptian torpedo boats were in motion, so that it was impossible for them to plant the explosives. As a result, Operations Escort and Raviv were pushed back until September 7 and 8, respectively.

Operation Escort 2: The Sinking of the Torpedo Boats in the Northwestern Gulf of Suez (September 7, 1969). The operational methods and force composition that were utilized in Escort 1 and 2 were basically the same. At around midnight, the pigs located the two Egyptian torpedo boats in a sedentary position near the southern edge of the area that they were assigned to comb. All eight of the limpets were planted and "non-removal" mechanisms were attached to the bottom of the vessels, which detonated the explosives and sank the boats.

On the way back to Sinai, a "self-destruct" mine that the force was carrying inadvertently went off on one of the pigs due to a defect in the device's engineering structure, and killed three of the four crew members. The fourth commando continued to look after the bodies of his dead comrades, despite being badly wounded himself. After treading water for over six hours, the surviving operator and the three bodies were pulled out of the water by a heli-copter unit. (See Chapter 3 for a comprehensive account of this operation.)

As planned, Operation Raviv—the landing of the armored force—followed on the tail of Escort 2, and the tanks caught the enemy completely off guard. The IDF commander in chief and the admiral of the Navy sub-sequently dispatched warm letters of commendation to the Shayetet's com-mander and the soldiers that took part in the planning and execution of the difficult operation. In addition, they expressed their deep sorrow over the loss of the three commandos.

Over the course of the four months that preceded the cease-fire agree-ment with Egypt in August 1970, the IDF once again revised its field regula-tions in the Egyptian theater. During this period, there was a general decrease in *MaShAG*—the Hebrew acronym for prevention, impairment, warning, and retaliation—operations. From that point on, ground combat missions relied on helicopter transports and IDF forces eschewed direct confrontations with the enemy. On the other hand, aerial attacks on the Egyptian front lines in-tensified. These included strikes against the anchorages at Hurgada and Ras Banas, which came in response to the Egyptian attacks on the port of Eilat and *Orit*, an Israeli fishing boat. These air raids, inter alia, replaced the aerial means that were hitherto at the disposal of the S-13 (parachuting into the sea and shuttling forces in helicopter pylons), as these methods were found to be inadequate. What's more, the arrival of maritime tools that suited the S-13's operations in this zone (such as *Snuniyot,* Bertram race boats fitted for combat use) was delayed because of procurement problems.

DEVELOPMENTS IN THE SHAYETET FOLLOWING OPERATION ESCORT

Despite the shift in the general trajectory of IDF operations, the General Staff frequently sent the Shayetet on infiltration operations and clandestine patrols behind enemy lines in all the theaters of action. For instance, the Shayetet began to conduct raids against terrorist organizations in Lebanon after the cease-fire agreement with Egypt (August 8, 1970).

The S-13's unique operational advantages and accomplishments started to seep into the consciousness of the Israeli public, and many new recruits were interested in serving in our ranks. Similarly, the reform of the training

Development of the S-13's operational activity from 1968 to 1969

*The assortment and magnitude of the unit's operations gradually increased.
*Improvement in the execution and quality of its military strike.
*Increase in the responsibilty and authority conferred upon the S-13 command.

Classic small-scale naval warfare.	Infantry missions executed by a large force under independent command.	Independent infantry operations carried out by a small force; clandestine surveying; and maritime demolition.	Helped infantry units cross water barriers and took part in the actual missions.	Independent, small-scale traversal of water barriers.

*The IDF acquired a new combat system.

Development of the S-13's operational activity from 1968 to 1969.

route, the reorganization of the combat units, and the new equipment that began to arrive bolstered the morale of the Shayetet's existing staff, many of whom—both officers and operators alike—decided to extend their service. As a result, the S-13's combat force climbed from thirty-two soldiers in May 1968 to seventy by 1971.

Each of the Shayetet's three major operations in the War of Attrition—Adabiyah, Green Island, and Escort—represented an arm of the unit's operational triangle. Although the objectives of the missions were rather similar, namely the liquidation of enemy troops and the destruction of installations, the characteristics and surroundings of each target were unique. Accordingly, the infiltration methods, nature of warfare, and combat means that the operators availed themselves of during each of the missions were different: Adabiyah, a defended compound on the coast, was breached by commandos who swam to the combat zone; Green Island Fortress, a defended compound in the middle of the sea, was infiltrated by a large group of divers who then engaged in conventional infantry combat; and the torpedo boats were reached by divers who advanced to within striking range on pigs.[10] Many of the techniques that were employed during these missions were recent innovations that helped distinguish the Shayetet 13 from other units in the IDF.

The standards that were forged by the S-13 and the diversity that in-formed its methods and missions during the War of Attrition engendered a panoply of combat skills and infrastructure that enabled the unit to conduct itself with ingenuity in every field of combat. Moreover, the Shayetet's perfor-mance during that period put the Israeli Navy on the "operational map." For the first time in its history, the Navy played an important role in a large and successful offensive, Operation Raviv. Consequently, the General Staff placed its trust in the Navy and granted it freedom of action in other campaigns, to include the Yom Kippur War.

TWO
The Raid on Green Island

Operation Bulmus 6

The raid on the Green Island Fortress was executed in July 1969, during the War of Attrition. Bulmus 6 was one of the most difficult and complex operations in the annals of the IDF, as well as one of the most studied and documented. The meticulous, professional debriefings remained classified as "Top Secret" for quite some time. Moreover, the accounts that were published before the security classification was removed were largely based on gossip, rumors, and tendentious interests.

In 1987, the Navy's History Section, headed by Ms. Liat Lerer, published a paper (*The Black Booklet*) that depicted the operation in a comprehensive, precise, and detailed manner, down to the level of the individual combatant. Lerer's study is predicated on both the extensive debriefings, which were conducted after the operation with the participation of the Sayeret Matkal, and the assiduous research by the cadets of the S-13's company commanders' course, under the guidance of Lieutenant Colonel (Res.) Avraham Zohar, in his capacity as the representative of the IDF's History Department. Zohar's effort centered around the mandatory, written personal reports that were filed by every S-13 operator to participate in the mission.

The IDF's Officers Training School released another booklet about the battle in January 1995. This publication constitutes a part of the army's "lesson plan" on leadership and command to this very day. In addition to all the above-mentioned sources, the paper draws upon the protocols of a seminar at the Naval Branch of the Command and General Staff College on how the command echelons managed the battle and reached decisions.

In 1997, the book *Great Raids in History*[1] was published in the United States. The book purports to describe the nineteen most famous assaults over the last 400 years. The Green Island raid is the only Israeli operation included in that distinguished list. Over the past few years, the battle has also been discussed in the official organs of the American, Greek, and Polish armies.

In the ensuing chapter, I will offer a succinct account of the preparations for the operation at Green Island; the background of and reasons behind the mission; the various stages of the battle, and its impact on both the enemy and the development of the S-13. This account draws on the aforementioned sources and the author's own research, as well as my experience not only as the Shayetet's commander during that same period, but as the commander of the raid who also personally took part in the fighting at the fortress.

THE TARGET

Perched on a sliver of rock in the heart of the northern Gulf of Suez, about a mile and a half southwest of the Suez Canal, the Green Island Fortress was 89 feet wide on one side and 213 feet wide on the other. Including the outer guard post, the compound was 476 feet long. The British built the fortress in order to protect the southern entrance of the canal. The compound was surrounded by walls that seemed to protrude straight out of the sea to a height of at least 8.2 feet, and the outer edges of the fortress hugged the sea. In addition, most of the perimeter was encased in barbed wire. The northern section of the compound was 148 feet long. A bridge with concrete support pillars knifed its way out of the northern façade and led to a round, concrete guard tower, a "pillbox," which we referred to as the "radar tower."

At the time of the raid, the fortress housed about a hundred soldiers and was equipped with the following weapons: six dual-purpose guns, which were positioned on the roof (guns #1 and #2 were 37 mm, and guns #3–6 were 85 mm); a radar (that turned out to be a phony); and some twenty emplacements—fitted with medium and heavy machine guns or light cannons—were dispersed throughout the compound. The island was also within range of Egyptian heavy artillery, while battleships and combat jets were capable of coming to its aid within an hour.

THE BACKGROUND OF THE OPERATION

The introductory chapter discussed the general background of and reasons for the assault on Green Island. At this juncture, I will briefly survey the primary events and decisions that preceded the raid. The IDF incurred heavy losses along the length of the canal throughout the month of March 1969. On April 20, the S-13 dispatched a clandestine maritime patrol to reconnoiter the Green Island Fortress (Operation Lahav 32). The patrol was part of an inchoate plan for a possible amphibious assault. At the outset, we considered various types of operations, such as mining the compound's anchorage, an aerial assault, or an artillery bombardment. The patrol came within arm's length of the compound's outer walls and yielded the following fruit:

- Data substantiating our assumption that a ground assault could indeed be pulled off.
- A shelf plan that could be carried out under the right conditions, should the need arise.
- Correspondingly, the S-13 began to conduct training exercises and experiments for the purpose of developing suitable methods, special means, and battle techniques for a ground assault against this unique target. Maritime and land-based surveillances of Green Island were also carried out in May, albeit from considerable distances.

On May 13, the Sayeret Matkal laid an ambush along the canal, with the Shayetet's assistance. However, the force encountered difficulties, as an officer from the Sayeret was killed and the troops returned without having fulfilled the mission.

At this stage, the defense establishment decided to ratchet up the operations on the Egyptian front. Six days after the failed ambush, the Shayetet clandestinely surveyed the radar station on the Adabiyah peninsula, some 3.5 miles from Green Island. On June 20, the Shayetet attacked the radar station from the sea. The installation was heavily damaged and the entire Egyptian force at the site was liquidated. As may be recalled, this was the first ground raid in the history of the S-13 and the first assault of its kind (an amphibious assault) in the entire annals of the IDF. Moreover, this was the first IDF attack against a defended compound on the Egyptian front since the Six Day

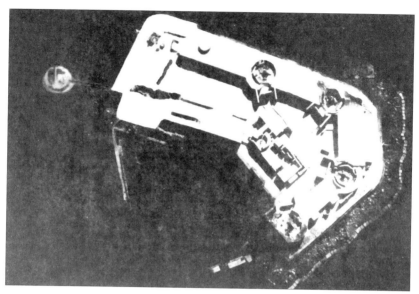

Bird's-eye view of the Green Island Fortress before the raid.

War, two years earlier. The mission's success bolstered the senior brass' faith in the S-13.

During a general-staff meeting on July 10, the commander of the 35th (Paratrooper) Brigade, Colonel Haim Nadel, submitted a plan for a raid against an Egyptian officers' club and medical corps base on the shore of Bitter Lake. The plan called for a combat force of over forty paratroopers to be transported on rubber crafts by the S-13. However, the IDF commander in chief Haim Bar-Lev had serious reservations about the plan's solution for Egyptian mines that were sprinkled along the lake's coast. Bar-Lev thus informed the units' commanders that he was transferring responsibility over the mission to the S-13, for it had "proved its ability to execute an infantry assault from the sea," three weeks earlier at Adabiyah. The confidence that the General Staff displayed in the Shayetet at this dignified forum induced me to advise Rear Admiral Avraham Botzer, the chief of the Navy, to propose to Bar-Lev (in a tête-à-tête, not before the full forum) a substitute for the Paratroopers' plan: the assault on Green Island. Botzer indeed presented the plan to the commander in chief, but he was not quite ready to give us the green light.

That same afternoon, the Egyptians raided the Pier Outpost at Port Tawfiq. Seven IDF soldiers were killed, five were injured, one was taken captive, and three tanks were destroyed. This attack, along with the Egyptian assault against the army's fortress opposite Ismalia three days earlier, set off alarm bells. In light of these developments, I once again proposed the idea of the raid on Green Island, only this time to the head of *Agam* (Operations Directorate), Major General David Elazar ("Dado"). The *Agam* chief was convinced that "cracking this sort of nut" would hammer home the message to the Egyptians that the IDF was not to be taken lightly and thus buttress Israel's steadily eroding power of deterrence. What's more, Dado took it upon himself to convince Bar-Lev to approve the mission and instructed me to begin training for the raid.

Besides the message of deterrence that we wanted to convey to the Egyptian army, the principal objective of the operation, I also preferred this particular mission for practical reasons. At the time, the Shayetet had only twenty operators who were adequately trained in infantry combat, while the Paratroopers' planned attack on Bitter Lake required over forty troops. Furthermore, although Colonel Nadel's Paratroopers had already invested over two months of training for the assault on Bitter Lake, we did not have enough time to prepare for that specific mission. On the other hand, we already had shelf plans for the assault on Green Island and conducted targeted experiments, drills, and observations that yielded special methods and means particularly suited for the operation. Likewise, we were well acquainted with the zone of operation due to the recon patrol and subsequent detonation of the terminal on the fuel island, the clandestine survey of Green Island, and the attack on Adabiyah. All these successes had galvanized the unit's confidence, and the combat level of our commandos was thus at a crescendo. Lastly, the S-13's collaboration with the Sayeret Matkal—especially its team commanders—was highly productive, so that we would probably be able to double our combat strength with twenty men from the Sayeret. In light of the above, I estimated that the Shayetet had the wherewithal to meet the challenge of the assault on Green Island.

On Saturday July 12, three weeks after the Adabiyah raid, the principal parts of the plan for the assault against Green Island were presented to Lieutenant General Bar-Lev. I was indeed appointed the operation commander, and the Sayeret was added to the mission as a complimentary force. This was followed by nine days of systematic training for the mission at hand. Over the course of the SOP, estimates of the situation were given on a daily basis and solutions were found for all the problems that arose. Likewise, the operational plans were updated in accordance with any additional information that arrived and in consequence of the results of our experiments and exercises. In March 1987, Commodore Ami Ayalon wrote the following account of these preparations:

> In retrospect, this was the best SOP that I ever participated in. The Shayetet's commander at the time, Ze'ev Almog, was involved in every last detail of the planning and preparations, and managed to allow the entire unit to participate in the planning and professional dilemmas . . . Details such as the direction of the approach, creating a diversion from the south, transporting the force, lists of essential equipment . . . were the topics of discussions . . . and [these matters] were settled over the course of the exercises that preceded the execution [of the mission].
>
> By the eve of . . . the operation, we were thus intimately familiar with every facet of the target, at least all the intelligence items that we could get our hands on, and we reached a perfect [level of] coordination and understanding of the scenarios, including how we were supposed to respond.[2]

THE OBJECTIVES OF THE RAID

The strategic goals of the Green Island raid were to bolster the IDF's power of deterrence and strike back at the Egyptians for their attack against the Pier Outpost on July 10. At the time, the Egyptians deemed the IDF to be a faint-hearted army that was largely dependent on American technology (including the recent addition of Skyhawk jets). We came to the realization that the best way to strengthen our power of deterrence was to prove the superiority of the storming Israeli *lochem* (warrior). The "cracking," as Dado put it, of a fortress as heavily defended as Green Island, which the Egyptians considered to be an impenetrable target, was meant to put the theories concerning the ostensible softness of the Israeli soldier to rest.

Given the psychological element of the mission's objective, we were surprised by the IDF General Staff's decision to launch an air strike on the heels of the raid against Green Island. The Air Force had hitherto focused on strikes deep within the Republic, but this time around it carried out its first massive bombardment of Egyptian positions across the entire length of the canal line (Operation Boxer) since mid-1967. The juxtaposition of the Green Island raid and the Air Force's offensive did not mesh. It appeared to obfuscate the IDF's effort to underscore the toughness of the Israeli *lochem*. What's more, the bombardment ran counter to the definition of a special operation, namely a mission that is conducted behind enemy lines with a relatively small force and limited means for the purpose of attaining a significant military and/or political objective.

Despite serving as the commander of the Green Island raid, I had no idea that a massive bombardment along the Canal Zone was even in the works. My immediate reaction was—and I still believe—that the juxtaposition of the two offensives was a tactical mistake because it created the impression that they were two inter-locking chapters of the same campaign, whereas in practice they contradicted one another, both with respect to the character of the missions and the goals that each was supposed to attain. In retrospect, it turned out that the consecutive operations nevertheless had a cumulative effect and led to the coveted change in the Egyptian mind-set, as the enemy finally came to recognize the superiority of the IDF.

PLANNING DIFFICULTIES

The Green Island assault was comprised of four stages: reaching the site; breaching the compound; mopping-up; and evacuation and withdrawal. All four phases contained problems that were known in advance and demanded solutions.

The Arrival Phase. The very location of the target (an island in the heart of the sea) made it difficult to reach and spawned the following questions: How would the force get to the island? How would we covertly transport a pair of combat groups—from different units and with divergent specialties—to the target in succession? The integrated operation, which would entail both diving activity and ground combat, placed limits on the amount of munitions that the force could avail itself of, for there was just so much weight that the divers could bear beneath the surface. Likewise, the water was liable to compromise the dependability of the weapons and ammunition. On the other hand, the waging of a ground offensive necessitated the haulage of a considerable amount of arms and appropriate webbing gear. Given the disparate facets involved, the operation demanded meticulous planning in all that concerned the equipment the commandos would take along and its reliability.

During the advance recon patrol on April 20, a maritime concrete signpost was located 460 feet to the south of the island. Strafing the enemy with heavy fire from the concrete post would facilitate the raiders' efforts to breach the target and gain a foothold, from which we could then conquer the entire compound. The roof of the maritime post was a flat surface that was susceptible to fire from the compound's southern wing. In order to take advantage of the signpost, we would have to come up with answers to the following questions: How would the detail get to the signpost? How would it position itself at the site in order to keep out of the line of fire? What would be the exact assignments of the detail on the site? And how would it communicate with the force's command echelon and the rest of the troops?

The Breaching Stage. The difficulties planning the breach stemmed from the following factors: the physical layout of the structure (a fortified and complex bloc); a profusion of troops stationed in tight quarters; the high level of alert at the compound; the ample munitions at the defenders' disposal; the large group of raiders assigned to the mission; their immediate transition from sea to land while catching the enemy completely off guard.

The Mopping-Up Stage. The target's physical layout was also certain to impede the force's efforts to mop up the fortress. The compound itself was comprised of a farrago of rooms, halls, and niches in which the defenders could hide. Moreover, there were about a hundred alert soldiers manning a host of emplacements, which were furnished with an assortment of machine guns and cannons. There were also the surrounding walls and a thicket of barbed wire fences. From the Egyptians' standpoint, the location of the target ruled out any prospects of escape, so that the defenders would have no choice but to fight for their lives. This predicament was likely to intensify the defenders' resistance, so that we would have to come up with an answer for these difficulties. In addition the target was surrounded by local defenses, to include heavy

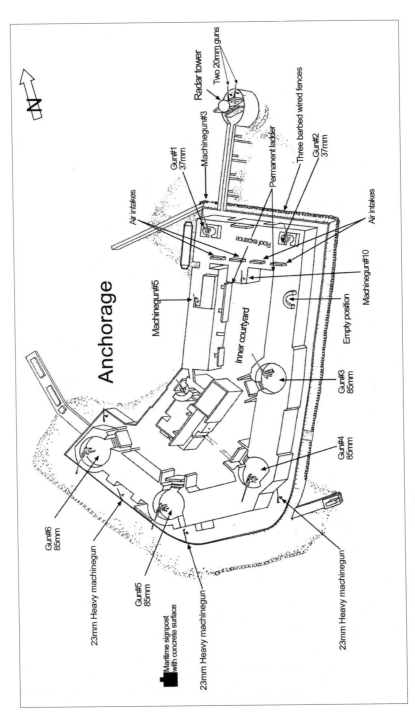

Positions and weaponry at the Green Island Fortress.

artillery, combat jets, and patrol ships. It was not out of the realm of possibility that these factors would fire at the island itself—once we had wrested control of it—and at our backup forces as well.

The Evacuation Stage. The withdrawal had to be carried out as quickly as possible, especially the evacuation of the wounded and the soldiers that had completed their role in the fighting. First and foremost, the evacuation would have to be meticulously organized, so that no one was left behind. Moreover, we examined the possibility that the Egyptians would strafe the evacuation route with artillery fire once they realized that we had no intention of holding on to the island, and the withdrawal was thus designed to minimize the exposure of troop concentrations to enemy fire.

While planning the operation, we were cognizant of the fact that the breaching, combat, and mopping-up stages would be hard-fought, complicated affairs which we deemed to be prerequisites for fulfilling the mission and limiting the number of casualties. With this in mind, we were guided by four basic principles during the planning and execution of the operation:

- Catching the enemy completely off-balance during the breaching stage.
- Maintaining constant pressure on the enemy throughout the course of the battle.
- Evacuating all the troops as early as possible and in an organized fashion. More specifically, the departure would be carried out in small and independent groups, so that each group would be free to move out as swiftly as possible.
- Sophisticated and efficient utilization of the S-13's special combat techniques, which were adapted to the unique conditions along the sea route to Green Island and in the compound itself.

We duly considered these guidelines to be prerequisites for fulfilling the mission and limiting the number of casualties

PLANNING AND PREPARING FOR THE MISSION

The planning process was informed by a great deal of "trial and error," at least until we managed to forge the appropriate techniques and methods. As is wont to happen in these sorts of situations, almost every solution that was found for a particular problem spawned new difficulties, which demanded yet another solution or response. In the end, the plan corresponded to the characteristics of the mission as well as the spirit of the four above-mentioned principles and their derivatives.

REACHING AND BREACHING THE TARGET

The plan of approach called for most of the troops to embark from Ras Masala in twelve rubber crafts. The combatants would be split into two forces: the Shayetet's "breach/grip force"[3] would consist of twenty soldiers arriving in five Mark V rubber crafts; and the Sayeret Matkal's "mop-up force" of twenty soldiers arriving on board seven Mark III crafts, along with a doctor, a medic, and the operation commander. The pair of distinct forces would be divided into two groups of boats, which would advance in an organized sailing formation, one group after the other, in a northerly direction, adjacent and parallel to the coast. The boats would stop about 1,750 yards from the target at the "Beacon Buoy," which would serve as a staging area and standby point. Both the sea route and deployment point were carefully chosen so as to ensure that the force would not be detected. In addition, a pig carrying three operators and weapons would depart from Ras Masala and proceed on its own to the maritime signpost to the south of the target.

While planning the approach from the staging area to the target, the Shayetet conducted an experiment. We attempted to shuttle the twenty members of the breaching force in three submerged pigs, with some of the passengers stretched out on the back of the vehicles. However, on account of poor visibility beneath the surface, we were unable to maintain a group formation of three pigs and the idea was abandoned.

Since avoiding detection until the target was infiltrated was a key to the mission's success, the rubber boats constituted the only feasible alternative for transporting forty commandos. This method would compel the members of the first wave to debark from the boats at a distance of at least 980 yards from the target, whereupon they would swim in concert for several hundred yards before diving the rest of the way. Due to visibility and control limitations, group diving is usually executed in single pairs, but under the circumstances all the divers had to reach the shore in one fell swoop. The simultaneous arrival was particularly critical for the final phase of the approach (the last 150 yards or so). With this in mind, we developed a new technique for twenty combat divers. The men were divided into pairs and contact ropes were inserted between all the divers' hands. Each pair's rope would be connected to a long cord in the middle. The submerged force would proceed on both sides of the central rope, so that their formation resembled a centipede. This complicated procedure was an absolute necessity for maintaining the force's cover before it penetrated the island.

In contrast, the Sayeret Matkal's commandos (who lacked the necessary diving skills) could only reach the target via rubber crafts. The crafts' approach to the target before the divers/raiders breached the compound was liable to compromise the covert nature of the operation and foil our chances of taking the enemy by surprise. Because of this, the decision was made to split the marauding force into two waves: the Shayetet's breaching and grip force, which would dive the final leg of the journey; and the Sayeret Matkal's commandos, who would arrive on board the rubber crafts and help the S-13 mop up the target.

One of the prerequisites for the mission's success was the storming of enemy positions and maintenance of constant pressure on the defenders throughout the entire battle. With this in mind, we drew up the following plan. Out of the twelve rubber crafts that would shuttle the entire assault force to the "Beacon" only a squadron of five Mark V crafts, carrying the members of the first wave, would initially approach the target. After advancing some two-fifths of a mile, the operators would enter the water and swim/dive the final half mile or so to the island. After the debarkation, the five boats would return to the standby position next to the buoy, where they would wait, along with the Sayeret's troops, until the first wave's commander summoned the second wave to join the fray.[4]

Problems were liable to arise on account of the seam between the two forces. As a result, the second wave's progression was divided into two separate stages:

- Upon receiving word from the commander of the grip force that the infiltration phase was under way, the second wave would advance to within 500 yards of the target.

- Upon receiving word from the commander that the foothold was secure, the second wave would link up with the first.

MUNITIONS

While planning the operation, the decision was made to have the rubber boats shuttle additional ammunition, demolition material, and communication devices throughout the course of the battle. This marked the first time in the Shayetet's history that twenty operators were slated to dive in tandem to a target. As a result, it was incumbent upon us to upgrade the dependability of the operators' equipment, pieces, weapons, and ammunition.

Special webbing gear was manufactured and outfitted to every relevant member of the Shayetet. The webbing allowed every diver/commando to simultaneously don both diving and infantry combat kits, including weapons and ammunition. The infantry kit was fastened to the chest, while the scuba set was strapped onto the commando's back with the help of new straps. The breathing set's tubes and the mouthpiece were routed over the head, so that the mouthpiece could be readily inserted into the mouth. The divers were supposed to remove the scuba equipment at the foot of the target, while still underwater, and thread their scuba gear onto the central contact rope. This measure would allow the boat operators to retrieve the sets in an efficient manner during the evacuation stage. The "hooves" (small scuba fins) were to be taken off the sneakers and strapped on to the diver's thighs by means of small rubber bands that were attached to the webbing gear, where they would remain until the end of the battle.

The water resistance of the arms and ammunition was of particular importance. In consequence, we ultimately adopted the following solutions to bolster the dependability of the munitions and the troops' confidence in them:

- The operators would use Kalashnikov rifles and Uzi submachine guns, both of which were proven to be dependable after diving when wrapped in nylon.
- The ammunition—bullets and grenades—were insulated by the Israel Military Industries Company and the Ordinance Corps. (Although the insulation withstood the test of our pressure cabins, the operators had problems with the hand grenades during the operation.)

For instance, the second wave was instructed to "reduce the range to 500m after receiving [Dov's] report that the fence is being breached"

Points of emphasis in Ze'ev Almog's final briefing paper before the operation.

- We procured small Dutch grenades that were conducive to waterproofing. Moreover, due to their compact size, the commandos could store a large quantity of the grenades inside their webbing.
- RPG bazookas and Bangalore breach charges were wrapped in water-resistant, nylon carrying cases, which were adapted for underwater haulage by divers.

THE MARITIME SIGNPOST

The primary purpose of the "holding and diversionary force" was to divert the enemy's attention and pin down (not necessarily liquidate) its southern positions, for the purpose of facilitating the efforts of the breaching force to the north. In order to ensure its covert arrival, the detail would reach the signpost on a lone pig, as per the suggestion of Ilan Egozi. The pig would then be tied to the bottom of the post, on the side that was out of the defenders' view, and the force would be able to covertly assume their positions.

The holding force's objective was to neutralize the enemy's heavy machine guns on the southern wing. We calculated the tilt angle and trajectory of the Egyptian 85-mm guns and found that their shells did not pose a threat to the position. In addition, the holding force could cope with light fire by strafing the enemy nests with MAG fire and taking cover behind the concrete marker. Lastly, the detail was armed with a Belgian bazooka (war booty). By dint of its mechanic mechanisms, the weapon was waterproof and its range was also longer than a standard bazooka.

THE TIMING OF THE BREACH

Since the operation was predicated, inter alia, on the infiltration of divers, we had to take into account the local sea state. The arrival was ultimately planned for high tide, due to the reasons noted below:

- At high tide, the sea level was deep enough for the divers to edge right up to the fortress, whereas at low tide the inlet is shallow and exposed.
- Currents tend to calm down and change directions at high tide. Therefore, we assumed that the currents at this hour would not hinder the troops' arrival. With this in mind, the advance recon mission on April 20 was carried out at high tide, and our assumptions proved to be correct. (Incidentally, the same conditions also prevailed during the survey and assault of the fuel island, which is in the vicinity of Green Island.)

We did not find a detailed account of the currents around Green Island in the British Admiralty's charts. In retrospect, these currents are apparently the product of an irregular local phenomenon, which derives from the topography of the surrounding seabed and other variable local factors.

Since the divers were burdened with a double combat kit and forced to advance as a group in a cumbersome diving formation, they were allotted an ample period of time of two and half hours to reach the island from the debarkation point out at sea. H-hour—the designated hour for the target's infiltration—was 0030. At the latest, the penetration would be executed at 0130, when the tide reached its peak. This time frame also corresponded with the intention of confining the mission to the darkest hours of the night, for the break of dawn was liable to expose the evacuating and withdrawing troops to Egyptian artillery batteries.

THE PENETRATION

Deciding upon the exact point of ingress was one of the most complex problems that we dealt with during the planning phase. We had to find a location where the troops could immediately get on solid ground and wield their weapons. Thanks to the clandestine survey of the target, a moderate incline was discovered at the north wing of the fortress, which would enable the divers to spring out of the water and head straight for the area beneath the bridge. The ten pillars supporting the bridge would serve as a temporary hiding place for the men and provide them with cover. In addition, the troops would have enough room there to prepare for the breaching phase.

Once the force had situated itself at this infiltration point, it would have to contend with a pair of five-foot-high fences with vertical pricks and a concertina fence in between. Needless to say, the facile circumvention of this formidable barrier was critical to the mission's success, and there were several options at our disposal. Quietly and slowly cutting through the fence with wire cutters entailed certain risks. A small peep was liable to arouse the attention of a sentry, and all it would take was a well-placed grenade under the bridge to wipe out the entire infiltration force. Alternatively, the use of an improvised Bangalore breach charge, which was specially fitted for scuba missions, was dangerous due to the limited cover provided by the pillars and the troops' proximity to the explosion. Another possibility was discovered during a surveillance that was conducted from the Pier Outpost on the very morning of the operation: an opening on the western corner of the fence. Although machine-gun nest #3 (sporting a Goryunov medium machine gun) loomed right over the spot, it presented an interesting alternative.

In light of the problems that accompanied each potential infiltration point, we decided to keep all three options open until the first wave reached the fortress. Consequently, each commando would train his sights on a predetermined enemy position until the final decision was made. In the event that the force was detected, every commando would open fire on his designated target.

THE BREACH

In order to complete the breaching phase, the force would have to capture the entire expanse on the roof of the compound's northern wing—from the wall above the landing beach until the air intakes on the opposite end—to include all its gun emplacements. The seizure of this area, which constituted the foothold, was the key to wresting control of the entire fortress. This stage presented the planners with several problems:

- The roof was nearly eight feet high. In consequence, the following solutions were contrived in order to mount the roof from the pavement:
  - The breaching troops would hoist themselves upon the shoulder of a particularly stout soldier. The soldier who was chosen for the job was Jacob Pundik, who thereby earned the nickname "Jacob's ladder."
  - Depending on how the battle unfolded and as per the discretion of the grip force's commander, the rest of the breaching force and the second wave would reach the roof via one of three routes: through the hall or the rooms in the northern wing and the courtyard; around the northwestern corner; or via the roof (like the conquest detail).
- There were a door and eleven windows on the north wing's façade, from which Egyptian soldiers were likely to emerge and offer resistance. However, there was no intelligence as to whether the area behind the door and windows consisted of a hall, or a series of rooms. As a result, we ultimately decided on the following two-pronged solution:
  - A member of the breaching team, Israel Gonen, would run across the length of the pavement and throw grenades through the windows.
  - A detail would be charged with mopping up the area inside the building. Upon completing this task, the detail would join the fighting on the roof.

- There was reportedly a radar on the island, but according to intelligence it was an air control device lacking surface-search capacities. Therefore, the primary danger that the radar tower posed to the first wave was the possibility of being visually spotted by sentries stationed therein, as the structure was located at the end of the bridge and was outfitted with a pair of 20-mm guns. During the advance recon patrol, it was impossible to discern whether a radar antenna was being operated on the island. We did know, however, that the Egyptians did not always activate their radars. The decision was thus made to cluster the rubber crafts into one bloc, about 1,700 yards away from the target (at the Beacon Buoy), so that they would form a spurious echo on the island's ostensible radar screen.

MOPPING UP

Our working assumption was that the force would be able to overcome this heavily armed and complex target by applying incessant pressure on the enemy through the following means:

- A covert entry; taking the initiative upon breaching the target; and securing a foothold on the roof of the northern wing.
- Reducing the seam between the first and second wave.
- Relentlessly charging enemy positions from north to south, starting with the northern and central section of the roof; followed by the length of the inner courtyard; and concluding with the destruction of the remaining positions on the southern part of the roof.
- Coordinating the actions of the holding force—the detail on the maritime signpost—and the first wave, so that the former could provide the latter with a succession of backup, holding, and diversionary fire from the moment the target was breached until a foothold was established. Likewise, the details fighting in the courtyard and those fighting on the roof would also coordinate and provide backup for each other.

EVACUATION AND WITHDRAWAL

The entire evacuation would be coordinated by a single officer (Dani Avinun). Our chief concern during the withdrawal phase was the Egyptian artillery, which covered the entire northern part of the Gulf of Suez. In order to prevent the troops from being exposed to artillery fire, the evacuation would be executed no later than 0230, so that the mission would not extend into the daylight hours. The departing boats would head directly to Ras Sudr, instead of Ras Masala—the embarkation point—which was within range of the nearest Egyptian artillery units. Moreover, we would scatter the withdrawing troops over a large area by dividing them into groups of two to four rubber crafts. Unlike large and cumbersome sail formations, this sort of arrangement would allow each boat to evacuate quickly, without the need for central control by means of wireless communications. In addition, the departing boats would be loaded in accordance with their standard capacities, so as to keep track of the number of evacuees.

The wounded were to be evacuated throughout the entire battle, in order to prevent a concentration of troops that would be susceptible to Egyptian artillery attacks. They would be tended to immediately at the collection point (the point of entry), and their treatment would continue throughout the ride back to the Sinai coast.

Several of the planning difficulties stemmed from within the ranks of the IDF command. To begin with, Raful, the chief Infantry and Paratroopers officer, objected to using tracer bullets during the operation because he feared that they would constitute a target for the Egyptian artillery. However, Menachem Digli and I felt that the use of tracers in a built-up area as complex as the Green Island Fortress would improve "the safety of our troops." We also contended that in any event tracer bullets were already included in the ammunition that would be fired by the holding force on the signpost. What's more, the Egyptians always lit up the sky when they were attacked at night, so that the tracers wouldn't stand out. Menachem and I presented these arguments to the commander in chief, who accepted our view.

On the third day of SOP, we put in a request for the Air Force to conduct an aerial photograph sortie, for the purpose of verifying and supplementing the information on the target. However, the General Staff was worried that the air patrol would reveal the IDF's intentions and turned down our request. We held our ground, and the recon flight was ultimately executed. In fact, the sortie revealed thirteen medium machine-gun, heavy machine-gun, and light weapon positions that we were previously unaware of. These new emplacements indicated that the Egyptians were not only on the alert for air strikes, but were suspicious of a surface offensive as well. Additionally, the recon flight discovered "bunnies" (hidden dugouts within emplacements), which necessitated the formulation of precise measures for mopping up these positions.

COMMAND AND CONTROL

The linking up of two assault forces, each with its own commander, obligated us to divide the responsibility between the two waves well in advance. Accordingly, I assumed command over the second wave for the following reasons:

- A commander with maritime experience was needed to preside over twelve rubber crafts.
- Critical decisions would probably have to be made during the approach to the target. Therefore, a good rapport and shared language between the commander of the second wave and the S-13's officers leading the first wave was instrumental to the linkup's success.
- In all likelihood, someone would have to coordinate between the breaching and holding force, which were shooting from opposite directions.

Once the second wave joined the battle, there would be nine sub-groups operating in the field. Consequently, we decided to set up a small-scale command post for the purpose of orchestrating this complicated enterprise. This command post would be comprised of the author, in my capacity as mission commander; Menachem Digli, the commander of the Sayeret Matkal; Dov Bar, who headed the first wave; and Uzi Livnat, a member of the first wave who would double as a signal operator. Upon reaching the island, I was to make my way to the edge of the northern roof (with a communication device for Uzi), where Dov would greet me with a report on the battle's progress. From that point on, the operation would be managed from the command post, which was to be located adjacent to gun position #4, at the center of the expanse.

In addition to the multi-branched communications system that was set up in conjunction with the General Staff's Signals Regiment (to include an airborne relay), I placed a lookout and communications post on the high tower of the "Quarantine," which was situated to the north of Ras Masala and in the general vicinity of the target. The post was operated by the Shayetet's signal officer and a reserve combat soldier ("Metukah"), both of whom were familiar with the operation's plan and the soldiers in the field.

EXERCISES

The training was an integral part of the SOP, and the exercises were regularly adopted to correspond with the operational planning, experiments, and additional intelligence information that filtered in.

Targeted exercises were primarily held by the S-13, and included group diving and movement in pigs and rubber crafts. The Shayetet and Sayeret Matkal held joint (no fire) exercises next to the Atlit Fortress, where we worked on linking up between the two waves. Each unit held its own drills on combat in built-up areas. Moreover, joint model exercises were carried out by the two units at the Mijdal and Gesher "police stations" (training compounds that were originally built by the British during the Mandate). During the final drill at Gesher, the Jordanians shelled the area. A squad commander from the Sayeret was wounded and replaced by Captain Ehud Ram, who later fell in the battle over Green Island.

Three incidents transpired on the very eve of the assault that had a direct impact on the mission. During the final briefing, the chief of the General Staff, Haim Bar-Lev, instructed the troops to retreat if they "sense" that the Egyptian resistance is too stiff. Additionally, Bar-Lev noted that "ten losses would be tantamount to the mission's failure." In my estimation, it was inappropriate for Bar-Lev to thrust the decision over whether or not to withdraw from the target onto the shoulders of the executing echelon. The latter is obliged to stick to the mission through thick and thin and lacks the authority to call for a retreat. Only the command echelon is authorized to make such a call, for only it possesses the operative and moral responsibility to decide, in advance, whether a mission is justified and if the force is capable of executing it; and if so, at what cost.

From my perspective, the commander in chief's remarks concerning the number of losses that would serve as the barometer for the mission's success were even more severe, and Raful and I were concerned about the effect that Bar-Lev's words would have on our men. Consequently, we sought to "reinterpret" his message in our closing remarks to the troops: "If we don't want to 'sense' that the Egyptians' resistance is 'too stiff,' and if we wish to avert losses, we absolutely should not stop charging or putting pressure on the enemy! Any pause in the offensive or . . . withdrawal before the enemy has been paralyzed is liable to cause numerous losses."

The second incident involved a convoy of two semitrailers, each of which was hauling a pig to Ras Masala. The trucks, which were directed by the commander of the tank troop in the sector, mistakenly entered a mine field near the Pier Outpost. One of the semitrailers set off a mine and was disabled. Furthermore, Senior Chief Petty Officer Meir Rabinovich, the commander of the technical department, was blinded. The second truck arrived safely, and its pig was ensconced in a camouflaged dugout at Ras Masala for safekeeping until the mission.

The third development, which was touched on earlier, occurred on the morning of the operation. Raful and I reconnoitered the target from the Pier Outpost and noticed an Egyptian motorboat approach the compound from the northwestern corner of the fortress, where it proceeded to unload equipment or people. We reached the conclusion that there must be an entrance or passageway at the northwestern tip of the fence, near the edge of the pavement. Hitherto, the plan had been to breach the target by either cutting or blasting a hole in the fence, but the new intelligence would enable us to unleash the initial charge on enemy positions with only minor delays and disturbances.

OPERATION ORDER

Out of the array of considerations, assessments, experiments, and drills, a general approach gradually took form. This approach was eventually translated into the operation order:

a. The IDF intends upon raiding Green Island.

b. On the night of July 19–20, 1969, the Navy will destroy the enemy force on Green Island and incapacitate structures and guns positioned on the island.

c. The mission will be executed by forty combatants: twenty combatants from the Shayetet and twenty combatants from an elite reconnaissance unit who will reach the target on twelve rubber boats.

d. H-hour—0030 commencement of the target's breaching.

e. Rescue force:

- Two helicopters and a doctor at Ras-Sudr.
- Bertram boats for defending against naval assistance.

f. Artillery support—a gun battery.

g. Air support—the Air Force will be on standby for an aerial rescue, offense action, and flare illumination.

h. Special instructions:

- Final hour for commencing the offensive action—0130.
- Final hour for leaving the target—0230.
- Force B will not approach the target until it receives word that the foothold has been seized.
- It is desirable to take 2–3 prisoners.

Several of the instructions that appear in the operation order demand further elaboration:

- According to the order, "the Navy will destroy the enemy force on Green Island and incapacitate structures and guns positioned on the island." Obviously, the term "to destroy" did not refer to the physical annihilation of every last enemy soldier on the island. From a military standpoint, destruction entails paralyzing the enemy until it is unable or unwilling to offer resistance. Therefore, our aspiration was to knock out as many of the defenders and positions as possible, but it was not necessary to literally kill *all* the soldiers and capture every last room or gun nest in order to fulfill the mission.

- The order stated that the force was to "incapacitate structures and guns." This, however, did not obligate us to destroy every last guardpost. The actual amount of damage to be inflicted was left to the discretion of the soldiers in the field.

- Under the headline "Special instructions," the order stated that Force B (i.e., the second wave) would not approach the target before receiving word that the foothold was secure. In other words, the deployment of the second wave was predicated on the progress of the first (the only phase that was subject to a precondition in the operation order). The planned delay in the second wave's arrival stemmed from the need to maintain the marauders' cover and catch the enemy by surprise. As noted above, the Sayeret's final approach was to be rendered in two stages: upon receiving word from the breaching force's commander that his troops have begun to cut through the fence, the second wave would advance to within about 550 yards of the target; after being informed of the seizure of the foothold, it would then storm the island.

The operation order was grounded on three primary forces, alongside additional support teams. The primary forces were slated to operate in the following manner:

- *The first wave,* totaling twenty S-13 operators under the command of Lieutenant Dov Bar, would be divided into four details. After diving to the shore, the force would breach the target and capture the northern part of the fortress. Upon securing the "foothold," Dov would summon the second wave to the island.
- Before the infiltration, *a holding and diversionary detail,* comprised of three S-13 operators and led by Lieutenant Emanuel Paz, would leave the embarkation point on pigs and covertly reach the maritime signpost to the south of Green Island. Once the first wave commenced the breaching action, Paz's detail would pin down the enemy's southern positions with heavy fire. The holding action would continue until the detail received an order to desist from the grip force's commander (either over the wireless or by means of a two-star rocket).
- *The second wave,* consisting of twenty commandos from the Sayeret Matkal and headed by the commander of the mission, Commander Ze'ev Almog, would split up into three teams and reach the target on rubber crafts. After disembarking, the second wave would make its way past the grip area in order to mop up the rest of the roof and execute the demolition actions on the island.

FORCES AND MISSIONS

In sum, the combat force consisted of nine sub-units: forty combatants, divided into seven details, would fight at the target itself; another detail comprised of three operators would execute holding actions from the maritime signpost;

a force of twenty-four soldiers would operate the twelve rubber crafts, which were to transport the two waves and shuttle additional supplies to the target; and lastly, a doctor and a medic would be on call on board one of the boats.

The support groups included the following components: a rescue force of two helicopters was on alert at Ras Sudr, along with another doctor; a maritime support unit, in the form of two Bertram patrol boats, would defend the raiders against naval intervention; a gun battery would provide artillery support; and combat jets would be ready to conduct an airborne rescue, strafe enemy forces, or drop flare illuminations.

As per the plan, the combat troops would be divided into the following details:

- The S-13 "breaching detail," headed by First Lieutenant Ilan Egozi, was charged with breaching the fence under the small bridge. Thereafter, it would neutralize machine-gun position #3 and then secure the northern part of the fortress until the evacuation.

- The S-13's "radar tower mop-up detail," led by First Lieutenant Gadi Amit (Kroll), was slated to clear out the radar tower. It would then join the fighting on the roof and cover the force's withdrawal during the final evacuation phase.

- Before joining the fighting on the roof, the Shayetet's "mopping up the compound's northern building detail," under the command of First Lieutenant Amnon Sofer, was responsible for mopping up the hall and the rooms to the north.

- The S-13's "capture of the expanse on the northern roof detail," headed by Lieutenant Dov Bar (the commander of the entire grip force), was slated to mount the roof via Jacob Pundik's shoulders, whereupon it would split up into two teams. One of the groups, under the command of First Lieutenant Ami Ayalon, was charged with clearing out machine-gun position #10 and gun position #2, while Dov Bar's sub-group contended with gun position #1 and machine-gun position #5. Dov also had to inform the "holding force" when to halt its fire and invite the second wave to join the fray (after it had already edged to within 550 yards). With the arrival of the second wave, Dov and Uzi Livnat (the commando/signaler) would link up with Lieutenant Colonel Menachem Digli and the author. The four of us would then run the command post from the roof.

- After covertly positioning itself on the signpost south of the island, the Shayetet's "holding and diversionary detail," which consisted of two combatants and a commander, Lieutenant Emanuel Paz ("Paulin"), would set up a Belgian bazooka and two MAG machine guns on the roof. As soon as the breaching phase got under way, the detail would open fire on the compound's southern positions until it received an order from the grip force's commander to hold its fire.

- "The roof mop-up and gun incapacitation detail" of the Sayeret Matkal, under the command of Captain Ehud Ram, was slated to link up with Gadi Kroll's team on the roof, whereupon it would proceed to mop up the roof's southern positions (#3, 4, 5, and 6) and disable the guns. In addition, Ehud Ram's detail was charged with detonating the guns after the battle.

- After reaching the roof, the Sayeret Matkal's "mopping up of the rooms in the courtyard's western wing detail," headed by First Lieutenant Chanan Gilutz, would descend from the expanse on the northern roof to the inner courtyard, via a ladder to the west, and clear out the rooms along the western side of the courtyard.

- The Sayeret Matkal's "mopping up of the rooms in the courtyard's eastern wing detail," under the command of First Lieutenant Amitai Nachmani, was slated to climb down the eastern ladder to the inner courtyard, where it would clear out the rooms along the eastern side of the courtyard. Moreover, it was supposed to link up with Ehud Ram's detail and cover the troops clearing out positions #4, 5, and 6.

- Lieutenant Commander Shaul Ziv and his deputy, First Lieutenant Dani Avinun, commanded a force of twelve rubber crafts, which was primarily responsible for transporting the forty combatants, who would be divided into two waves of twenty combatants each. The first wave would be ferried in five Mark V rubber crafts and the second wave in seven Mark III rubber crafts. Over the course of the battle, the force would also deliver ammunition and explosives to the combatants; retrieve the first wave's equipment; help evacuate the casualties and whisk them back to Sinai; and organize the evacuation in groups of two to four rubber boats, while keeping track of the number of evacuees.

GREEN ISLAND—THE SHAYETET'S EXCLUSIVE TASKS

- Breach the target and seize the critical space for the foothold.
- Pin down the southern positions on the roof with fire from the maritime signpost.
- Transport and evacuate all the combatants to and from the target.
- Supply ammunition and explosives over the course of the operation.
- Evacuate the equipment of the casualties from the target.

Although the job was originally allotted to the Sayeret Matkal, the S-13 also exclusively handled the demolition assignment at the compound following the hostilities.

EXECUTION OF THE MISSION

The Approach toward the Target. The Green Island Fortress was located in the very center of the Gulf of Suez's northern "head." On Saturday night, July 19, 1969, the combat forces assembled at the battle's forming-up point in Ras Masala, southeast of the target. The troops were divided into three forces: the S-13's "breaching/grip force," which would dive to the island and infiltrate the compound; the Sayeret's "mop-up force," which would reach the target in rubber boats; and the Shayetet's "holding and diversionary force," which would debark on board a pig and operate from the maritime signpost.

The first to exit Ras Masala were the three members of the holding force. A half hour later, at 2030, the twelve rubber crafts—the largest operational force ever to be marshaled under the Shayetet's command—set out on the mission, setting a northerly course for Green Island. The force was divided into two groups, which maintained a distance of 110 yards from one another. In order to avoid detection, all the boats kept close and parallel to the Sinai coastline. The Shayetet's grip force was transported in five Mark V rubber crafts, which were arrayed in an arrowhead formation and formed the vanguard of the small fleet. They were followed by the Sayeret's mop-up force, whose seven Mark III rubber crafts were aligned in a diamond formation. My own boat, from which I navigated the entire force, accompanied by Raful, Shaul Ziv, and the commander of the first wave, Lieutenant Dov Bar, constituted the tip of the arrow. At 2150, after advancing 3.5 miles, the boats changed direction opposite the

Quarantine Tower, assuming a northwesterly course to the staging area next to the Beacon Buoy. Ten minutes and 3.2 miles later, we turned west, and all boats were gathered around the Beacon by 2222. All that remained between the force and the island was a mere 1,750 yards.

The first wave then received a warning to get ready to enter the water. Soon after, the breaching force's five Mark V rubber crafts cautiously proceeded, under my command, to the dipping point. At 2245, the twenty commandos slipped into the water. Exactly fifteen minutes later, following a brief staging, they began to swim in concert toward Green Island, and the five boats returned to the Beacon. At this point, I transferred to Menachem Digli's boat, while Raful and Shaul Ziv remained in place. The boat that I boarded was tied to the buoy, and the rest of the crafts were subsequently attached to moored boats, so as to prevent them from drifting off to sea during the long hours of waiting that were in store for us.

In the meantime, the holding force had navigated its way to the maritime signpost. It reached the concrete, 13 x 13–foot-wide structure at 2300, some two hours before the first bullet was fired. The pig was moored to the post's southern wall, which was concealed from the enemy's three 85-mm guns and three heavy machine guns in the compound's southern wing only 150 yards away. At the stroke of midnight, the three operators—Emanuel Paz ("Paulin"), Aryeh Yitzchak ("Aryo"), and Avishai Ben-Yosef—climbed the metal rungs that were nailed into the post's southern façade and positioned themselves on the narrow roof, some 6.5 feet above the water. The two MAG-58s and munitions cases were set up on both ends of the surface, and the Belgian bazooka was situated in the middle. At 0024, six minutes before H-hour, Paz reported that his force was ready. However, the threesome would have to wait another forty-five minutes or so before commencing its fusillade on the enemy's southern defenses.

THE GRIP FORCE'S APPROACH

After 65 minutes of westward group swimming, Dov realized that his force was advancing at a slower than expected pace on account of unanticipated currents. Consequently, Dov decided to switch to diving at 0005, but the progress under the water was rough, as the operators found themselves breathing heavily and sinking under the burden of their ammunition. Those at the end of the

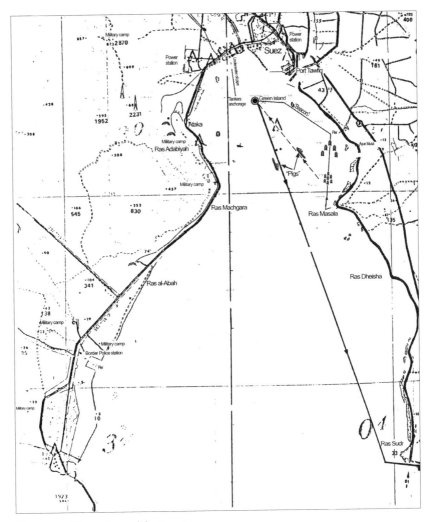

Movement of forces toward the target.

line had a hard time gauging their depth and plummeted forty feet below the surface.[5] At 0030—the predetermined H-hour and sixty minutes before the final deadline for opening fire—Dov surfaced and discovered that the force was still over a third of a mile southeast of the target. The commander summoned all his troops to the surface and excoriated them to gird their loins and swim against the current in a northwesterly direction.

During this time, Raful and I tried to contact Dov three times, but didn't receive any response. We thus had no idea how the first wave was faring or where it was. Under the circumstances, the second wave would not approach the target without Dov's clearance before the 0130 deadline, as any attempt to hasten the approach was liable to imperil the grip force.

In any event, by 0110, the force had advanced to within 165 yards of the radar tower's northern tip. At this point, the operators took up their positions along the length of the central cord and submerged, whereupon they began their final approach at a depth of over sixteen feet, just above the seabed. Dov took a peek above the surface after advancing another 150 yards and was able to make out the radar tower. Thirty yards later, Dov stole another glance. At this point, he could already see the sentry stationed on the northwestern corner of the roof and another guard in the middle of the pavement.

Amnon Sofer, the commander of the detail charged with mopping up the northern hall, had his goggles and mouthpiece knocked off his face by the fin of the diver in front of him when he was about 100 yards from the target. As per the guidelines set in advance, Amnon had no choice but to tread water until the fighting began. As a result, he was temporarily replaced as the detail commander by his deputy, First Lieutenant Gil Lavie.

BREACHING PHASE

Dov Bar finally laid his hand on the radar tower at 0125, whereupon the troops were instructed to remove their scuba equipment. Five minutes later, they were ordered to mount the muddy and tar-stained inlet under the radar tower, with Dov and the breaching detail, headed by Ilan Egozi, leading the way. The first wave began to deploy, as per the planned alignment, in the small space beneath the bridge and behind the pillars, while every commando trained his weapon on a designated position. Under Ilan's command, First Lieutenant Yossi Zamir and Petty Officer First Class Israel Dagai prepared a Bangalore breach charge and placed it on the fence for possible detonation. The detail then began to silently cut a hole through the fence. Meanwhile, Ilan clearly identified the opening at the western end of the pavement that Raful and I had sighted from the Pier Outpost on the morning of the operation, and brought it to the attention of his men.

At 0130, the aforementioned final deadline for breaching the target, Raful took another stab at contacting the members of the breaching force, but they still were not listening to their communication devices, even though they had reached dry land. What's more, Raful's attempt to make contact through Paulin, who was recumbent on the maritime signpost, also failed.

By 0138, the last members of the first wave were already deployed on the ground. An Egyptian soldier suddenly appeared on the pavement waving a flashlight and heading in the direction of the men cutting the fence. Ilan immediately opened fire and killed the sentry. His detail then rushed toward the opening at the tip of the gate, while holding their fire. Upon entering the fortress, they attacked machine-gun position #3 and liquidated its defenders with small-weapons fire. The Egyptians reacted with inaccurate fire, which sailed over the commandos' heads; as expected, they also activated the search-lights. During the initial charge, Ilan was hit by grenade fragments in both legs, but fought on.

SEIZURE OF THE GRIP AREA[6]

The seizure of the grip area—the expanse on the northern roof—on the part of the first wave was deemed to be critical to the mission's success. As per the plan, which was devised and drilled in advance, the foothold was established in three stages, the first of which included the following steps:

- At the outset, Petty Officer First Class Israel Asaf, who was positioned at the end of the line of the advancing commandos, launched rockets from his RPG into the radar tower located above him. Israel then sprinted over to machine-gun position #3 (fitted with a Goryunov), which was presumably liquidated by Ilan Egozi's detail. However, he spotted an Egyptian soldier hiding inside and took him out. From the emplacement, Israel fired his RPG at gun position #6, which was situated atop the compound's southern wing, on the far side of the island.
- Once the target had been breached, Petty Officer First Class Israel Gonen, a member of the breaching detail, ran eastward across the length of the pavement while threading grenades through the windows of the building to the north. Heeding the plan, Gonen stopped at the northwest corner of the pavement in order to secure the building's eastern wing.
- First Lieutenant Gadi Kroll also passed by machine-gun position #3, before climbing onto the bridge and storming the radar station, which was seated atop a round structure and contained two 20-mm guns. With

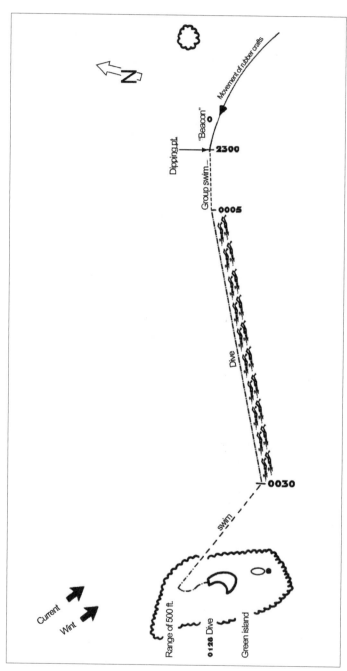

Movement of the grip force toward the objective.

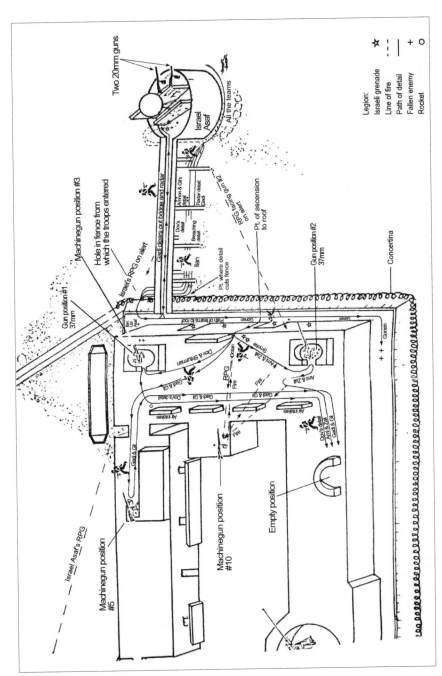

Breaching and grip phase.

the help of cover from his troops, Gadi liquidated the two Egyptians who were stationed in the position. In addition, he discovered that the radar was a phony.[7]

- Ilan and Gadi's details essentially neutralized the main sources of heavy fire in the front of the fortress and surmounted their initial obstacles. These actions enabled Dov Bar's detail to advance eastward along the pavement and reach the designated spot from which the troops would ascend the roof. Concomitantly, First Lieutenant Gil Lavie (who replaced Amnon Sofer as detail commander) and his four commandos prepared to burst through the front door of the northernmost building, in order to mop up its inner expanses.

- As soon as Ilan Egozi had pulled the trigger beneath the bridge, the holding force on the maritime signpost opened fire on the compound's southern emplacements. To begin with, they launched a bazooka rocket that hit the southeastern side of the fortress. Thereafter, Avishai Ben-Yosef unleashed his MAG on the enemy, primarily focusing on its heavy machine guns. These actions drew an immediate response from the Egyptians: an illuminating bomb, which was unfurled from gun emplacement #5, lit up the surrounding area, and the improved visibility enabled the enemy to return accurate fire from its southern positions.

The Shayetet's commandos were charged with completing the physical conquest of the foothold during the second stage. In other words, the first wave endeavored to ascend the roof and take control of all the positions on the expanse up to the air intakes on its southern edge. Ami Ayalon, Dov's deputy in the "conquest detail," was the first to mount the roof (via Haim Shturman's shoulders, and not Jacob's ladder in this instance). Upon reaching the ledge of the roof, Ami threw a smoke grenade, but the device did not work and a spark grazed his forehead. Ami tried another grenade—this time an explosive—which also failed to go off. Nevertheless, Ayalon ascended the roof with Petty Officer First Class "Zali" Roth right behind him. In the face of fire from machine gun #10, which cut through one of Zali's fingers, the tandem stormed gun position #2. Ami managed to quell the source of fire, whereupon the two raiders proceeded to clean out position #2. Petty Officer First Class Shimon Dotan, who climbed the roof after Ami and Zali, fired an RPG rocket toward that same machine gun that Ami had just silenced. Dov Bar and Chief Petty Officer Haim Shturman subsequently ascended the roof and mopped up gun position #1, while receiving cover from Ami and Zali, who fought on despite his injury.

While Ami and Zali were in the process of clearing out emplacement #2, two Egyptians escaped from the position and scrambled down to the pavement. However, they ran into Israel Gonen, who managed to kill both soldiers. This stage of the battle came to a close when Gil Lavie's detail stormed into the northernmost building. Petty Officer First Class Motti Greenman burst through the door and then stayed in place, for the purpose of securing the entrance. The rest of the detail charged inside, where they found an empty—and rather spooky—columned hall, which did not contain a door or passageway to the inner courtyard.

Upon cleaning out the northern hall and radar tower, respectively, Gil Lavie and Gadi Kroll's details headed to the roof to help complete the conquest of the foothold. Meanwhile, Ilan Egozi (notwithstanding his injury) and Greenman stayed below in order to guard the northern walkway, alongside Jacob Pundik. Jacob was also slated to serve as a human ladder for the Sayeret force, which was due to arrive at any moment.

The third and final phase of the foothold's establishment entailed, inter alia, the following actions. Gadi and Gil stormed machine-gun position #5 at their own initiative and wrested control of it. However, they did not notice the Egyptian hiding in the dugout (bunny) that was buried inside the emplacement, and he would subsequently make his presence felt. Gadi and Gil then linked up with Dov Bar next to the rightmost air intake, on the side closest to the "empty nest." At this point, all the members of the grip force that had climbed to the roof assembled around Dov and opened fire on the southern emplacements.

Aryeh Yitzchak ("Aryo"), a member of the holding force, fired his bazooka, but the powerful recoil knocked him off the maritime signpost and into the sea. This surprising incident interrupted the detail's succession of fire and enabled the Egyptians to intensify their own fire. Consequently, the three members of the holding force were forced to scramble off the roof and take cover behind the post. At 0145, the fire tapered off a bit and the three men returned to their positions. As my boat was making its way toward the target, Paulin forwarded a request for permission to resume fire, and I gave him the green light.

Meanwhile, Dov Bar finally sought to make contact with the mop-up force. His wireless was out of order, so Dov launched a green rocket, which was the alternate signal for the second wave to join the fray. However, at my behest, the second wave had already left the Beacon the moment we heard the first crack of gunfire. When the flare went off, our boats were already about 650 yards from the target.

When Dov felt that the fire from the signpost was beginning to endanger the grip force, he fired a two-star flare, which was the holding force's cue to halt its fire. Having completed its mission, the holding force climbed down to the pig and awaited the order to withdraw.

Adhering to a structured and well-drilled plan, the conquest of the grip area ran like a well-oiled machine. Notwithstanding the fears of excessive casualties, the foothold was seized without any loss of life and only two light injuries to Ilan and Zali.

In order to prevent the enemy from regaining its bearings (and in accordance with the guidelines set forth during the briefing), Dov decided to keep up the pressure on the enemy by deviating beyond the established borders of the grip area. More specifically, Dov endeavored to capture two more emplacements: gun position #3 and machine gun #5.

With this in mind, Dov dispatched Haim Shturman and Yoav Shachar to wrest control of machine gun #5. From there they would be able to pin down the enemy positions along the southern wing. On their way to the emplacement, Haim and Yoav were joined by Yossi Zamir. Dov was unaware of the fact that Gadi and Gil had already operated at this position. Due to the unrelenting combat, they did not have a spare moment to give their commander an update. However, even if Dov had been informed of their progress, he was still justified in sending out the team, for it was incumbent upon the force to reaffirm its control over that entire area. In any event, as Shturman and Shachar approached position #5, with Yossi Zamir covering their backs from the south, the aforementioned Egyptian soldier popped out of the dugout and tossed a grenade. Although Yossi subsequently managed to liquidate the enemy, Haim and Yoav were killed on the spot. Two boat operators, Petty Officer First Class

Yossi Kvashni and Petty Officer First Class Itzik Hurtz, who were already on the island, fulfilled their solemn duty by retrieving the bodies of their fallen comrades.

The logic that necessitated the maneuvers beyond the "official" boundaries of the grip area also applied to gun position #3. Accordingly, Dov dispatched Ami Ayalon, Didi Ya'ari, and Zali Roth to capture that emplacement. After mopping it up, the three men were joined at the position by Gadi Kroll, Gil Lavie, Israel Asaf, Israel Dagai, and their commander, Dov Bar.

THE SECOND WAVE OF THE SAYERET MATKAL JOINS THE FRAY

When the final hour for breaching the target—0130—came and went, and we had yet to hear from Dov Bar, it was clear that something had gone awry. However, I didn't find a definitive answer in the debriefing material as to why Dov deviated from the plan and failed to provide us with so much as a word about his progress. Did Dov simply forget to activate the communication device due to the pressure he was under? Was he afraid that the senior brass would order the troops to pull out because the deadline had elapsed? Or perhaps, he simply wanted to minimize the noise so long as his troops were right under the nose of the guards and had yet to breach the compound? All we know is that Dov clearly made no attempt to activate the communication device before ascending the roof. Therefore, the second wave of the Sayeret Matkal didn't have the slightest clue as to the fate of the breaching force, or whether to proceed with the intermediate phase of the silent approach (i.e., the advance to within 550 yards of the target). The second wave would not have enough time to draw closer if it remained at the buoy, but we ultimately decided to stay put, lest a premature advance give away the mission and imperil the men of the first wave.

As soon as the first bullet was fired at 0138, the second wave detached from the buoy and darted toward the island, without waiting for Dov's request. Instead of the six to seven minutes it would have taken us to reach the island from the designated point about 550 yards from the target, the excursion from the Beacon took seventeen minutes. Consequently, the linkup between the two waves was delayed by nine to ten minutes. We paid a price for this toward the end of the battle, when the Sayeret's details were unable to exert enough pressure to pin down or liquidate gun positions #4, 5, and 6.

Seven minutes after the fighting commenced in the compound, Emanuel Paz ("Paulin"), the commander of the holding force, who also failed to make contact over the wireless with Dov, asked for my clearance, as mentioned above, to resume fire (after his detail had managed to return the roof). Paulin's request came in as I was making my way at top speed to the island, along with the rest of the second wave. From my vantage point on the lead boat, I had an unobstructed view of the entire length of the fortress and could thus see that the fire from the signpost would not endanger the grip troops for the time being. Moreover, I assumed that if Dov lacked wireless communications, he would not be able to ask the holding force to resume its fire. On the other hand, should the need arise, he would be able to order Paz to desist by means of a flare. I therefore approved of Paz's request to strafe the enemy's southern positions.

Three minutes later, at 0148, we spotted Dov's green flare calling upon the second wave to enter the battle. A two-star rocket was sighted immediately afterward, which was Paz's signal to hold his fire.

As the second wave was making its final approach, the motor of the rubber craft that Digli and I were on began to shudder and the boat lost speed. I screamed to the rest of the boats to "Keep moving and don't split up!" Although this minor glitch compelled our boat to bring up the rear, we nevertheless reached the target together with the rest of the force.

By 0155, all the boats had reached the island, and the Sayeret's three details, headed by Ehud Ram, advanced according to plan. All the members of the second wave passed through the breach, whereupon the entire mop-up force made its way along the pavement toward the point of ascension to the roof.

While the Sayeret Matkal's troops began to mount the roof, the Shayetet's grip force was cleaning out gun #3 and machine gun #5, with the exception of Dov Bar and Uzi Livnat who were waiting for me on the ledge of the roof. I handed over the communication device to Uzi, who assumed the role of mission commander's signaler and was right at my side until the battle ended. I then stretched out my hand to Digli from the edge of the roof in order to help him on, so that he could join us, as planned, in the command post. However, he turned down my assistance and said that he would climb up on his own. I turned away and that was the last I would see of Digli until the evacuation phase.

Dov gave me a rundown of the situation and I got the impression that the Egyptian resistance was weak. I then immediately advanced along with Dov and Uzi toward gun position #4, from where we would preside over the rest of the battle, as well as all the evacuation, demolition, and withdrawal actions. As we passed the empty position on the way to position #4, we came across Ehud Ram's detail and I urged them to pick up the pace.

At 0200, only five minutes after the second wave had reached the roof, the General Staff's tactical headquarters, which was located on the shore of Ras Masala, started to put pressure on us to wrap things up, even though the evacuation deadline was 0230. I reported back that "two-thirds of the target is in our hands. We will carry on until the mission is complete!" As soon as I got off the line with headquarters, I was informed that Shachar and Shturman had been killed.

After Ami, Didi, and Zali had captured gun position #3, the former proposed to seize control of gun position #4 together with Kroll, Lavie, Asaf, and Dagai. Dov took Ami up on his offer, before proceeding to the northern edge of the roof for our above-mentioned meeting and to instruct the Sayeret's combatants to advance to their targets via the designated ascension point on the roof.

In the meantime, the five Shayetet operators set out to capture position #4. They were met by heavy fire from its defenders, but refused to back down. Ami and Gil stormed the emplacement, while Didi, Asaf, and Dagai covered them from above. The sixth commando, Gadi Kroll, waited on the edge of the roof next to gun position #4, where he was scheduled to meet up with Ehud Ram and provide him with an update of the proceedings. A sniper took aim at the team from gun position #6, and Didi was hit on the leg. Dagai fired back and Asaf tried to stymie the position with his bazooka. His first attempt was off the mark, but his second rocket hit the emplacement and silenced it for the time being. Suddenly, a grenade was hurled from the 23-mm heavy machine gun below and to the east of gun position #4. All five commandos were injured, the worst being Didi, who was badly wounded in the stomach. The only one to stay out of harm's way was Gadi, who was situated between the source of fire and his five comrades-in-arms.

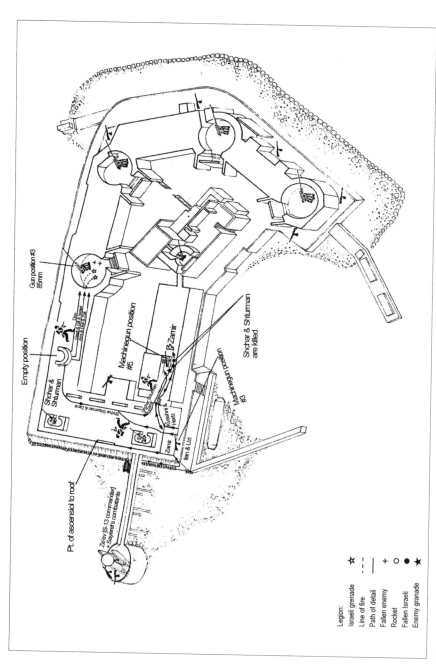

Gun position #3
85mm

Empty position

Shohar &
Shturman

Pt. of ascensiol to roof

Zeev [S-13 commander]
Sayeret's combatants

Machinegun position
#5

Zamir

Machine-gun position
#3

Shohar & Shturman
are killed

Legion:

☆	Israeli grenade
- - -	Line of fire
———	Path of detail
+	Fallen enemy
○	Rocket
●	Fallen Israeli
★	Enemy granade

Mopping up gun #3 and machine gun #5.

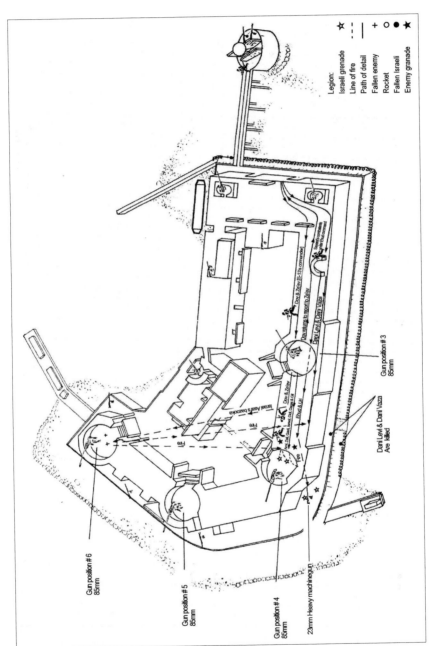

The Sayeret joins the fray, and the S-13 operators in the fight for gun #4.

The second wave started to get into the thick of things. As the Sayeret's Ehud Ram and Uri Matityahu made their way to the meeting with Gadi near gun position #4, Uri tossed a phosphorus grenade at the underlying heavy machine gun. Thereafter, Uri noticed that his detail was left behind and was forced to turn back. He then moved his troops to gun #3 before rushing back to Ehud, in order to cover him while he received a report from Gadi. Toward the end of the meeting, Ehud was hit in the head by sniper fire from position #6 and was instantly killed. Ehud was immediately replaced as the mop-up force's commander by his deputy, First Lieutenant Uri Matityahu.

At this stage, Dov, Uzi, and I reached the commandos at gun position #4, where I witnessed Ami incur his third injury of the day—this time to the neck, while persisting with his and Gil's efforts to neutralize gun position #4 and the machine-gun nest below. In addition, I got a firsthand look at our casualties, including the body of the Sayeret's fallen commander, Ehud Ram, and ordered Gadi, who was unscathed, and Uzi and Dagai, who were slightly injured, to evacuate the casualties. Ami informed me, in a hoarse voice, that he would leave on his own.

Although there were no eyewitnesses, the fire from gun position #6 also appears to have ended the lives of the Sayeret's Dani Vaza and the S-13's Dani Levi. In light of the fact that their bodies were found on the outer pavement encompassing the eastern wall, they were probably hit while storming gun position #4 and fell off the ledge of the roof.

While the casualties were being removed from the roof, two Egyptians appeared at the end of the courtyard beneath the command post and attempted to flee to gun position #5. Dov and Zali—who in the meantime had joined us at the command post—and I fired at them from the roof and both were liquidated.

After the mission, we tried to ascertain the reasons behind the complications at position #4. We reached the conclusion that the difficulties stemmed from the fact that the S-13's breach force did not stop with the seizure of the foothold, but hastened to storm gun positions #3 and 4, despite lacking any semblance of fire cover. According to the plan, the Sayeret Matkal's troops were supposed to engage these two emplacements. However, they arrived late so the Shayetet's men fought by themselves in both positions. Although the

S-13's men displayed an exemplary level of perseverance and determination, they lacked the holding action and cover to contend with the fire from the most remote enemy positions on the roof. Upon storming gun position #4, the commandos ran into a firetrap—primarily in the form of bursts from gun #6 and the 23-mm heavy machine gun under #4—while operating on a surface that was essentially bereft of cover and concealment. As a result, they were exposed to three primary sources of fire: gun #6, gun #5, and the 23-mm heavy machine gun beneath position #4. What's more, there was no backup whatsoever, as the holding force on the maritime signpost to the south was already forced to desist and the Sayeret's details were still operating in the courtyard and thus could not exert pressure on the enemy's active gun nests and maintain continuity of fire. Alternatively, the Egyptian soldiers that manned these positions had no means of escape and thus found themselves with their backs to the wall. The only option that remained open to them, short of throwing in the towel, was to intermittently pop up from behind their cover and snipe at our troops.

At 0210, the General Staff's tactical headquarters ordered me to stop fighting. The most distant position, gun #6, was already completely silenced, but gun position #5 was still offering resistance. Notwithstanding the order, I felt that it was incumbent upon us to finish the job and instructed Uri Matityahu and Amnon Sofer (who in the meantime had rejoined the force after losing his goggles) to continue with the assault on position #4. For the second time, Uri returned to his detail, which was located at gun position #3, in order to bring them to the command post. On their way back, Uri's commandos riddled gun #4 and the underlying heavy machine gun with gunfire and grenades. The lid was blown off of both positions on account of the ammunition inside, and an Egyptian soldier stumbled out of one of the nests engulfed in flames. With that, position #4 had finally been silenced.

Under the cover of Uri's detail and the men at the command post—Dov, Zali, and I—Amnon and Uri reached the edge of gun position #5 and threw phosphorus grenades inside. The explosion set off the ammo shells within the emplacement, and the entire nest was transformed into a wall of fire. Uri and Amnon ducked for cover behind a stack of sandbags, while the position's three defenders were catapulted through the air, whereupon I ordered the team to pack it in.

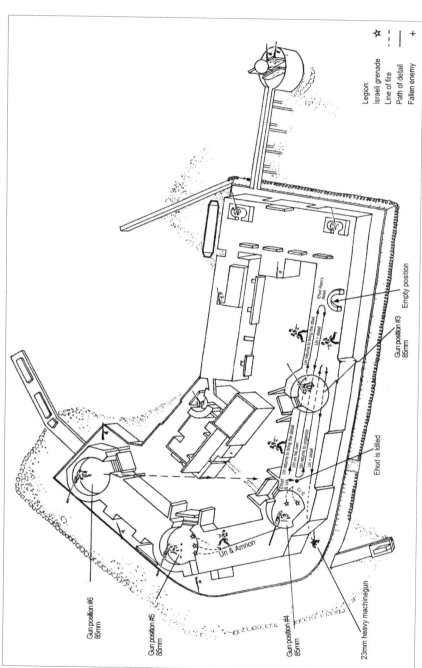

Fighting at gun positions #4 and #5.

Legion:
☆ Israeli grenade
┊ Line of fire
— Path of detail
+ Fallen enemy

Gun position #6
85mm

Gun position #5
85mm

Gun position #4
85mm

23mm heavy machinegun

Uri & Amnon

Ehud is killed

Gun position #3
85mm

Empty position

Ehud Ram's detail

Uri returns to bring the detail

Uri on his own

Uri returns to organize

Uri + detail

Uri returns to bring the detail

Uri + detail

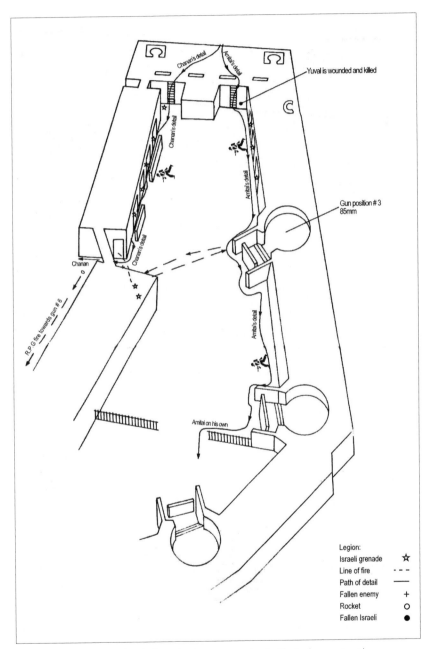

Amitai's and Chanan's details from the Sayeret waging battle in the courtyard.

By 0215, the enemy was completely paralyzed. Two minutes later, at 0217, I notified Raful, who was listening in on the radio from the boat, that the troops had been ordered to begin the evacuation. Raful then relayed the information on to the General Staff's tactical headquarters.

As noted above, three details from the Sayeret Matkal had ascended the roof (via Jacob's ladder). One of them remained on the roof, while the other two sought to make their way from the roof's northern expanse to the eastern and western sides of the inner courtyard, respectively, by means of permanent metal rungs that were set in the concrete wall.

First Lieutenant Amitai Nachmani's detail found the eastern rungs and headed down to the courtyard. The commander was the first one down the ladder, followed by Shai, Yoram, Boaz, Nimrod Viz'anski, and Yuval Miron. The latter two then bypassed the others, whereupon Nimrod came across and killed an Egyptian soldier. Amitai fired and threw a grenade into the room on his left, but the shrapnel injured Yuval and Nimrod (the rest of the detail was protected behind cover). Boaz dressed up his wounded comrades, before rejoining the detail, while Nimrod remained behind to tend to Yuval, who was in bad shape. However, Nimrod's foot was crushed and he was losing a substantial amount of blood. Nimrod quickly realized that he would not be able to remove Yuval without assistance, but managed to evacuate on his own by climbing back up the ladder.

The second room along the route of Amitai's detail was locked. A grenade was thrown inside, but none of the troops entered the room. After mopping up the third room, Amitai advanced to the area beneath position #3, where he was scheduled to meet up with Ehud Ram. Amitai called out for Ehud, but no reply was forthcoming. At this point, Amitai's troops encountered resistance from the headquarters building across the way, and they returned fire. However, First Lieutenant Chanan Gilutz, the commander of the Sayeret's detail that was operating on the opposite end of the courtyard, clamored for Amitai to disengage, lest his own men get caught in the crossfire. Gilutz's troops then managed to neutralize the enemy fire. In the meantime, Amitai's detail reached the area beneath gun #4. Amitai then continued on his own through an opening in the fence along the southern edge of the courtyard, where he happened to see the aforementioned trio of Egyptians hurtling out of position #5. At that point, he received the evacuation order and started heading back.

After finding the ladder on the western side of the courtyard, Chanan Gilutz's detail conducted themselves quite differently from their counterparts across the way. Before leaving the roof, the commandos threw a grenade into the first room in the courtyard. Only then did they climb down the metal rungs, under the cover of the detail's bazookist, who led the way. However, the detail ran into problems right off the bat. In the first room, they had difficulties with the weapons and had to replace them. From our position atop the roof, we witnessed Chanan's men run into fire as they approached the second room. However, they immediately countered with fragmentation and phosphorous grenades, which enabled them to eventually clean out the room. Rooms #3 and 4 were sealed, and Chanan tried to force his way in by firing and kicking at the locks.

At this juncture, the detail was nearly caught in the aforementioned fire-fight between the enemy in the adjacent rooms and Amitai's detail to the west. Chanan's men subsequently fired their weapons and tossed a phosphorus grenade through the window. For good measure, they also tossed several fragmentation grenades on the roof and subsequently managed to clear out the rooms. Chanan identified a declivity under the window, which led to the basement and generator room. He fired and tossed a grenade into the basement. Upon receiving the evacuation order, the troops heard a faint mutter coming from the generator room, and Noam and "Cookie" were ordered to go in and investigate. They found an Egyptian hiding behind the generator, who they managed to silence. In the meantime, Nachum had been positioned at the rear by his commander in order to cover the detail's advance. He fired his bazooka at gun position #6, but the rocket streaked over the position. Before he had a chance to launch another rocket, the evacuation order came in and Nachum withdrew.

At 0215, Digli appeared on the northern expanse of the roof, opposite the command post. By that point the enemy was no longer showing any vital signs and the evacuation order had already been issued. Digli, the commander of the Sayeret, was brandishing a megaphone with which he called on the Egyptians to surrender in Arabic. I called out to Digli to start evacuating his men. Thereafter, the members of the command post turned their attention to rescuing and tending to the injured, evacuating the remaining equipment, and preparing the demolition sets for detonation.

THE BOAT FORCE

After detaching from the Beacon, the five rubber crafts, which had shuttled the grip force to the diving point under the command of Shaul Ziv, linked up with the seven rubber crafts under the command of Dani Avinun, who transported the Sayeret to the fortress. As planned, Dani orchestrated the entire boat force. His team of operators was responsible for, inter alia, the following diverse assignments:

- Regularly supplying ammunition to the members of the first wave, which at one point nearly ran out.
- Stacking 80-kg packs of demolition near the northern entrance to the fortress.
- Collecting the scuba equipment that the breaching force left at the foot of the bridge.
- Filling the withdrawing boats with the standard number of passengers (as opposed to a personalized list). This activity started the moment the first rubber crafts reached the island and continued until the end of the mission.

Two boat operators, Yossi Kvashni and Itzik Hurtz, evacuated Didi, who was badly injured, and Shturman's and Shachar's bodies from the target. Another operator, Gidi, and Benny Azulai, the medic, retrieved Dani Vaza's and Dani Levi's bodies. The rest of the injured soldiers were assembled at the debarkation point and were sent off in groups of at least two rubber crafts. At 0225, the first group of wounded soldiers was ferried back, along with the Shayetet's doctor, Dr. Shimon Slavin, who tended to his patients throughout the return trip.

The Evacuation from the Target

As soon as the fighting abated, the evacuation from Green Island got under way. The entire process lasted 38 minutes, from 0217 to 0255, nearly as long as the battle itself (39 minutes).

By the time the evacuation order was given, the compound's defenders were paralyzed and did not even attempt to disturb our efforts to leave the island. That said, the threat of an Egyptian artillery barrage hovered menacingly over our heads. Consequently, only those combatants who were charged with securing the evacuation, assisting in the withdrawal of personnel and equipment, or executing the demolition remained on the island after the fighting had subsided.

The details of the Sayeret and Shayetet evacuated the target on boats, in the same fashion they had arrived. Chanan (the commander of the Sayeret detail that mopped up the western rooms) ordered his men to open fire, hurl grenades, and launch a pair of RPG rockets at the anchorage and pier from machine-gun position #5 for the sake of securing the evacuation of his detail, which had not suffered any injuries.

The post-battle removal of casualties was conducted at two foci: the courtyard, where Yuval Miron lay wounded; and the pavement outside the compound's eastern wall, where Dani Vaza and Dani Levi had fallen. Amitai's detail, Digli, and I lifted Yuval up the ladder to the roof with the help of a rope and escorted him to the north side, where he was lowered to the pavement via Jacob's ladder and carried off to the boats. Digli and Uri Matityahu, who combed the roof and the area along the pavement, located Vaza and Levi on the lower pavement between gun positions #3 and 4. Reaching the bodies, however, turned out to be quite a challenge due to the steep incline and concertina fence. I ordered Dani Avinun to dispatch a rubber craft, which reached the bodies by circumventing the fortress from the east. Gidi, the medic, and Uri Matityahu, who maneuvered through the adjacent barbed wire with wire cutters, helped the boat operators extricate their fallen comrades.

Lastly, the holding force returned to Ras Sudr on its own on board the pig.

THE FINAL EVACUATION AND DEMOLITION

After Chanan's detail withdrew, Gadi Kroll replaced them at machine-gun position #5 and secured the evacuation on his own. He then descended to the northwestern pavement, where he eliminated two Egyptians, who were heading toward the anchorage and had emerged from behind the building. Upon finishing, he evacuated to the boats and sailed to Ras Sudr.

The demolition was supposed to be coordinated by Ehud Ram, but the Sayeret officer had been killed soon after his arrival. Since the 85-mm guns were heavily damaged during the fighting, we did not have to tend to these, or the phony radar. As per the plan, at this stage I put a premium on evacuating the wounded and reducing the number of soldiers on the island. The remaining members of the Sayeret were charged with evacuating Miron, Vaza, and Levi, while the Shayetet's cadre of officers (Sofer, Egozi, and Lavie), headed by Lieutenant Commander Shaul Ziv concentrated the explosive substance (a total of 80 kg) in the northern hall and prepared it for detonation. I decided not to plant explosives on the roof's cannons and medium machine guns on the assumption that razing the building would also incapacitate all the pieces that were perched on top of it. An object fell on Shaul's foot while he was inspecting the northern hall. He hobbled out of the building on his own, and I ordered him to board one of the boats. In the meantime, two Egyptian artillery shells landed near the pavement, adjacent to the four remaining rubber crafts, and one of the boats was hit in the stern. I thus urged Dani Avinun to evacuate all those who had completed their duties: Digli, Sofer, Uzi, and Gonen (the latter had secured the eastern pavement) departed on one boat, which was followed by Avinun, Shaul, Raful, and Ephraim Selah on a Mark V rubber craft. Thereafter, a lone Mark V on the foot of the bridge was the last available means of transportation on the island

The only men still in the compound were Ilan and Gil, who were finishing up the demolition work; Dov and I, who were collecting the miscellaneous equipment that was dropped by the wounded on the roof; and two boat operators, Moshe Tavlan ("Zusman") and Eyal Banai.

At 0255, the detonators were activated, and all the remaining soldiers headed down to the bridge. Only after we boarded the Mark V did I realize that Ilan and Gil were injured. We sailed a half mile to the east of the target in order to distance ourselves from the blast, whereupon we veered off to the north a bit—in the opposite direction of the withdrawal—for the purpose of returning to the south and confirming that the explosives indeed went off following the nine-minute delay. After the blast, we watched the Egyptian shells rain in on the fortress.

Sometime after the operation, Raful wrote an appraisal of our detonation and the subsequent Egyptian shelling: "I assume that all the Egyptians on the island were killed. It must be remembered that the Egyptians themselves also subjected the island to a severe bombardment. . . . [If] anyone remained alive after our operation and wasn't killed afterwards in the Egyptians' shelling, it is indeed a miracle from heaven. In fact, I can declare myself to be an eyewitness. I left the target on the next-to-last boat. Thereafter, there was a heavy bombardment. Every meter of water was shelled."[8] Although we were the last ones to leave the island, we were happy—as well as somewhat surprised—to find that we were the first to reach the naval base at Ras Sudr. By the time we stepped off the boats, it was already 0415.

THE WITHDRAWAL

Except for the last two boats (my own and Avinun's Mark Vs, fitted with two engines apiece), each of which returned on its own, all the other boats were evacuated in pairs. Given the possibility that Ras Masala would be shelled, the entire force was instructed to head straight for the more distant Ras Sudr. Ras Masala was indeed bombarded at 0410, and the members of the General Staff's tactical headquarters, which was situated there, were forced to evacuate.

We took the following precautions in order to contend with the expected Egyptian artillery strike and avoid casualties, regardless of the source, during the evacuation:

- The evacuating boats were dispersed over enormous distances.
- We eschewed the use of communication devices or any form of central control, which was superfluous and could not have been sustained to begin with.
- Sailing safety was maintained by moving in pairs.
- All the pairs were free to move at maximal speed, so that none of the teams would be fettered by other boats.

The first four rubber crafts, which were reserved for injured soldiers and Dr. Slavin, had already left Green Island at 0225. After seven minutes, the boats were forced to split up. The two boats advanced slowly, so that the doctor could care for the soldiers during the trip and jump from boat to boat. Among the wounded was Petty Officer First Class David Kliot, the only IDF combatant to suffer a shrapnel wound during the Egyptian bombardment. The other

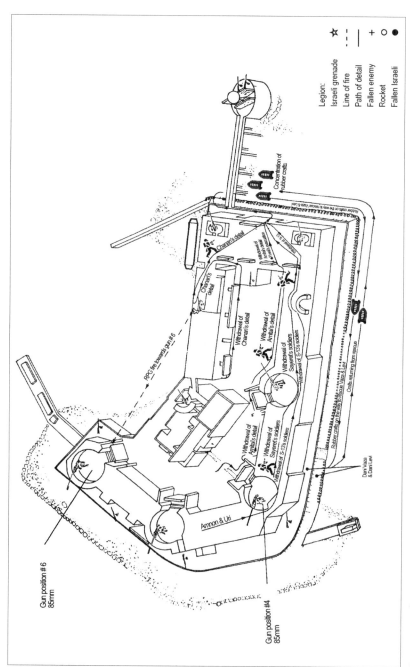

Evacuation of target.

Legion:
- ☆ Israeli grenade
- ┊ Line of fire
- │ Path of detail
- + Fallen enemy
- ○ Rocket
- ● Fallen Israeli

Gun position #6
85mm

Gun position #4
85mm

Amnon & Uri

RPG fire towards gun #6

Withdrawal of Charan's detail

Charan's detail

Withdrawal of Amital's detail

Withdrawal of Sayeret's soldiers

Withdrawal of S-13's soldiers

Withdrawal of Amital's detail

Withdrawal of Sayeret's soldiers

Withdrawal of S-13's soldiers

Concentration of rubber crafts

Rubber crafts on the way to rescue Vaza & Levi

Rubber crafts on the way to rescue Vaza & Levi

Crafts returning from rescue

Dani Vaza & Dani Levi

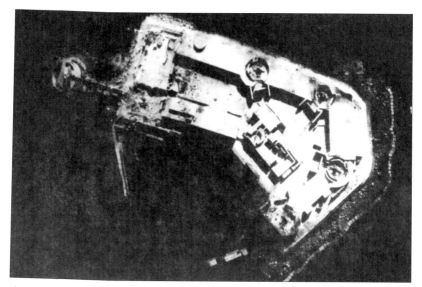

The Green Island Fortress after the raid (results of the demolition).

two boats requested and received permission to accelerate their pace and thus distanced themselves from the other two.

The last two crafts to leave the island in concert were the only "couple" that split up along the way. The boat that had been hit in the stern by a shell had engine problems and lost speed. Two of its passengers, Digli and another Sayeret commando, transferred to the second boat, which was carrying Vaza's and Levi's bodies. Several minutes later, the damaged boat came to a complete standstill, as both its motors turned over and sank into the water. However, Digli's boat neither stayed to accompany the sinking craft nor returned to the fortress to seek our assistance, even though its crew knew that we were still on the island, which was only about 300–400 yards and a three-minute ride away. Digli's craft did try to signal and catch up with Shaul's boat, but both efforts failed.

There were six men in the sinking boat: First Lieutenant Amnon Sofer, Amos Weiss, Uri Be'eri, Uzi Livnat, and Israel Gonen from the S-13 and the Sayeret's Uri Matityahu. Before bailing out, Amnon Sofer instructed everyone to inflate their life vests and take along their personal arms, a cartridge, a Motorola device, a "Sarah" homing device, and a jerrycan with five liters of water. Livnat and Matityahu then destroyed the rubber craft with their knives and

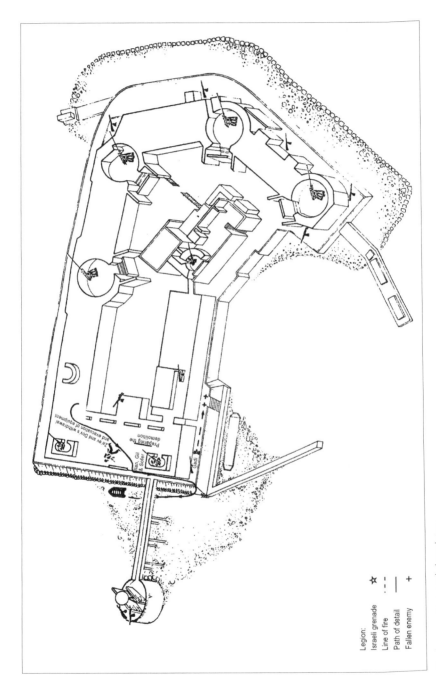

Final evacuation and demolition.

Legion:

Israeli grenade   ☆

Line of fire   · – ·

Path of detail   ——

Fallen enemy   +

set off flares and red sparks, but neither Shaul nor Raful noticed them. The six soldiers then began to swim eastward, in the direction of the Sinai coast.

The capsized crew did not manage to make contact with anyone until 0515, when the lookout and communications post that I positioned atop the Quarantine Tower, on the coast southeast of Port Tawfiq, picked up their call for help. The lookout team was comprised of Mike Kurkis, the Shayetet's GaNaK officer—a Hebrew acronym for detection, navigation, and communication—and a reservist, Eliyahu Schwartz ("Metukah"). After Kurkis passed on the information about the swimmers' plight and their coordinates to the IDF communication relay, they were located over 1,000 yards east of Newport Rock. At 0523, they received a warning that an enemy boat was heading toward Newport. The General Staff's tactical headquarters, which mistakenly thought that the men were located on the rock, notified them that a Bertram boat and fighter jets were being sent to engage the enemy boat and artillery was put on alert. Lastly, two choppers were dispatched to pull the swimmers out of the sea, and Dov Bar volunteered to accompany one of the helicopter crews.

The swimmers had already covered over two miles when they noticed the helicopters from afar. They immediately split up into a pair of threesomes and launched flares to attract the choppers' attention. During the first pass, the helicopters swept over Newport Rock, but the pilots had yet to turn on their Sarah receivers and failed to spot the troops. The choppers were immediately targeted by Egyptian antiaircraft guns. After turning south, they activated the Sarah and headed back in the direction of the swimmers. Under a hail of inaccurate shelling, they managed to collect all six men within a minute, and both choppers touched down at Ras Sudr by 0615.

Over the course of the withdrawal process, the rubber boat operators made several attempts to drop the wounded off at Ras Masala, but their requests were denied on account of the shelling. They were, however, permitted to debark at a beach to the south of Ras Masala, which was out of the range of Egyptian artillery batteries. In order to expedite the evacuation of the wounded and spare them the convulsions of the road, they were picked up by helicopters. Last but not least, one of the casualties, Petty Officer First Class Israel Asaf, was whisked off his boat by a helicopter in the middle of the sea.

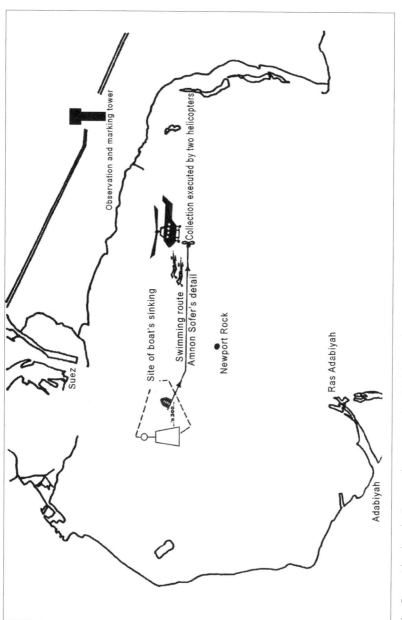

The Green Island raid—Rescue of swimming detail (rubber craft #9).

Results of the Raid

As a result of the assault, between seventy and eighty of the island's defenders were killed, including the victims of "friendly fire" during the Egyptian bombardment after the evacuation. The northern wing of the compound was razed and the six guns on its roof were incapacitated. Thirteen emplacements were eliminated and the rooms around the courtyard were cleared out.

On the other hand, six of our troops were killed: Dani Levi, Haim Shturman, and Yoav Shachar from the Shayetet; and Ehud Ram, Dani Vaza, and Yuval Miron from the Sayeret Matkal. Ten soldiers from the S-13 and one from the Sayeret were wounded. In addition, the technical manager of the S-13's pigs' department had been wounded the previous morning. All the IDF's combatants, around seventy in total, returned to base. Despite the heavy Egyptian artillery, no lives were lost during the evacuation and withdrawal from the target.

All the injured S-13 commandos returned to active duty. Two of them, Ami Ayalon and Yedidya Ya'ari ("Didi"), went on to command both the unit and the entire Navy. Shaul Ziv and Uzi Livnat also assumed the command of the Shayetet, while Gadi Kroll, Ilan Egozi, and Israel Asaf served as the unit's deputy commander.

Six S-13 commandos were decorated for their role in the battle: First Lieutenant Ami Ayalon received the Medal of Valor; First Lieutenant Gil Lavie the Gallantry Medal; and Lieutenant Dov Bar, Chief Petty Officer Zali Roth, First Lieutenant Ilan Egozi, and First Lieutenant Gadi Kroll were awarded the Distinguished Service Medal. I recommended the citations, in conjunction with the chief Infantry and Paratroopers officer, Brigadier General Rafael Eitan ("Raful").

Military missions are measured by the extent to which they fulfill the operation order. As may be recalled, the operation order of the Green Island raid called upon the Navy to "destroy the enemy force on Green Island and incapacitate structures and guns positioned on the island." Notwithstanding the unique difficulties involved—unexpected currents; the target's location in the heart of the sea; its complicated layout; the host of fortified positions, cannons, heavy machine guns, rooms, and defenders; the lack of escape routes for the enemy; and the abundance of enemy forces in the region—the mission was a complete success. The enemy troops that were stationed on the island

Soldiers of the Shayetet 13

| Haim Shturman | Yoav Shachar | Dani Levi |
| of blessed memory | of blessed memory | of blessed memory |

Soldiers of the Sayeret Matkal

| Yuval Miron | Dani Vaza | Ehud Ram |
| of blessed memory | of blessed memory | of blessed memory |

Soldiers that fell during the raid on Green Island Fortress.

were wiped out and structures were demolished. Once the battle was over, we controlled the target without any resistance whatsoever from the surviving defenders until every last member of the assailing force had left the island (a grand total of 38 minutes). In other words, the enemy at the target had lost the wherewithal and willingness to fight and was decidedly "destroyed."

Raful testified to the fact that the greater objective—strengthening the IDF's power of deterrence—was also attained: "The island could have been attacked from the air, but it was necessary to demonstrate to the Egyptians our superiority in face-to-face encounters, for . . . according to their way of thinking Israel's air superiority was merely a technical advantage. Even in

Citation recipients.

their worst nightmares, they couldn't have envisioned . . . such an audacious operation!"[9]

In his study, *The War of Attrition from the Perspective of Egyptian Sources*, Dr. Mustafa Kabha discussed the effect that the operation had on the enemy: "[Green Island] constituted a turning point in the War of Attrition. It symbolized the beginning of a new phase in the campaign, which most of the Egyptian scholars termed 'the stage of counter attrition,' in which the military initiative passed from the hands of Egypt to the hands of Israel."[10]

The methods and modes of battle as well as the novel techniques and means that were utilized in the Green Island raid established a high benchmark for quality and new combat norms. These assets became the bread and butter of the S-13's operations for many years to come. Below are some of the most prominent precedents: transporting forty combatants to a fortified target in the heart of the sea and nevertheless taking the enemy completely by surprise; infiltrating the target with twenty operators who swam and dove to the target in group formation, while logging a dual set (diving and infantry); the execution of a smooth and instantaneous transition from the water to ground combat "under the noses" of the Egyptian guards; the covert placement and coordinated operation of a holding and diversionary force that reached its position on board a "pig"; and qualifying combat gear, equipment, and munitions for divers, who upon emerging from the water used their cargo in ground combat.

Raful evaluated the mission from the standpoint of the IDF's professional standards:

> The execution of the Green Island raid was out of the ordinary in its exceptional success. . . . I believe that with this operation the IDF achieved an important accomplishment in its own right. This achievement is not momentary, for its importance [is not limited] to the fact that we invaded the island and conquered it, but [stems from the fact] that we blazed a path towards a new combat approach and contributed significantly to our self-confidence in our ability to operate and carry out complex and complicated missions, like the raid on Green Island. . . . Despite the heavy losses, we displayed a skill level that is likely to serve

as a milestone for many years to come. . . . We gained invaluable experience which will undoubtedly spare us from future losses in human life.[11]

Additional Perspectives on the Green Island Raid

At Green Island, the S-13 earned its reputation as an elite combat unit that doggedly adheres to the mission at hand and is capable of carrying out both maritime and ground-based raids alike. In the month and a half after the assault on Green Island, the unit executed three additional assaults, including the sinking of two Egyptian torpedo boats in Operation Escort, which paved the way for a successful armored landing and assault. What's more, the General Staff began to realize the need for a substantial increase in the Shayetet's combat strength.

The lessons, experience, and confidence from the assault on Green Island were put to good use in many subsequent operations. As a result, there was a significant drop in the number of casualties and the Navy's operational stock continued to soar. To wit: the Navy—in general and the S-13 in particular—repeatedly performed with distinction during the Yom Kippur War, while concluding the campaign with three losses (including two Shayetet commandos who fell during a commando raid on Port Said). Likewise, the Navy did not lose any troops over the course of the maritime antiterrorist operations following the Yom Kippur War, from April 1979 onward, to include Operation Peace of the Galilee (the First Lebanon War) in 1982.

The following section offers several other perspectives on the operation. These excerpts have been taken from speeches that my colleagues delivered as part of the aforementioned seminar, "Special Operations in the Wars of Israel from 1943 to 1981."

Lieutenant Colonel (Res.) Yossi Abboudi: The Background for the Force's Activities during the Period of Operation Bulmus 6. (Lieutenant Colonel [Res.] Yossi Abboudi served as the head of the Air Force's History Section). On July 20, 1969, the Air Force was ordered to attack Egyptian targets along the northern part of the Suez Canal. This was the Air Force's first offensive action after a two-year recess. Its previous strike in the canal was in July 1967, immediately following the Six Day War. Although the Air Force was subsequently involved in quite a few actions in Egypt—primarily intelligence missions, such an aerial photographing—it did not participate in any offensive activity along the canal. That said, the Corp took part in raids deep within Egypt and was active in other sectors along Israel's borders. There were several reasons for this:

- The Air Force lost 50 planes during the Six Day War. Until the beginning of 1968, it had only 150 combat jets. In contrast, the Egyptian Air Force had already returned to 80 percent of its prewar strength by October 1967, thanks to aid from the Soviet Union.
- France slapped an embargo on Israel after the war,[12] and no one knew if and when the sanctions would be relaxed. Offensive actions on the part of the Air Force were likely to exacerbate Israel's relations with France.
- On the eve of the Six Day War, Israel signed a deal with the United States for the procurement of Skyhawk jets. Consequently, there was concern that a show of air power in the Canal Zone would be considered a violation of the Israeli-Egyptian cease-fire agreement. This was liable to induce the United States to slap on an embargo of its own and trigger condemnations in the United Nations.
- The Air Force eschewed attacks in the Canal Zone out of a clear desire to avoid losses.
- There were fears that airborne operations along the canal would escalate into an "all-out war," which Israel did not desire.

Nevertheless, the decision to unleash the Air Force in July 1969 came in response to persistent Egyptian artillery fire. These attacks inflicted heavy casualties on the IDF, and no other way could be found to put an end to Egyptian belligerence. Furthermore, the Egyptians interpreted Israel's abstention from wielding its strong air force as a sign of weakness, which the IDF high command was eager to dispel. The reassertion of the Air Force into the canal front thus derived from Israel's desire to punish the Egyptian army (particularly its air force) for its artillery barrages against Israeli positions and reestablish its air superiority, at least in the region.

From April to July 1969, fourteen Egyptian planes were downed, but the Arab Republic continued to get embroiled in battles. After serious deliberation, the IDF General Staff decided to go ahead with Operation Boxer 1, an air strike against Kantara and its northern environs. The mission was carried out on July 20, 1969, and lasted from four in the afternoon until nightfall. The Air Force attacked two missile batteries, artillery positions, tank depots, and outposts. Furthermore, interdictions were conducted along the axes of the surrounding roads. Three Egyptian planes attempting to intercept our planes or hit Israeli targets in the Sinai and across the length of the canal, were shot out of the sky by IDF aircraft. Likewise, an Egyptian plane was downed by an MIM-23 Hawk missile and another was bagged by antiaircraft fire. In Boxer 1, the Israeli Air Force conducted a total of 250 sorties, all within the boundaries of the Canal Zone. Save for operations during full-fledged wars, this was the largest bombardment that the Air Force had ever carried out in a single day. Almost all the IDF's combat jets and every type of aircraft in its arsenal were used in the operation, to include the Skyhawk. Two of our Mirage jets were downed—one in a dogfight and the second by antiaircraft fire—but the pilots managed to parachute to safety in the Sinai peninsula.

The Air Force resumed its offensive actions four days later with Operation Boxer 2, which was also concentrated in the vicinity of the canal. The mission came on the heels of Nasser's July 23 speech in which he declared the launching of "the Bloodletting War" (or what Israelis refer to as the War of Attrition) against Israel and reaffirmed the well-known three "nos" of the Arab summit in Khartoum: no to negotiations with Israel, no to recognition of Israel, and no to peace with Israel. Operation Boxer 2 was similar to Boxer 1 with respect to the amount of sorties, the magnitude of the strikes, and the number and types of planes involved. However, this time around five Egyptian planes were downed in dogfights and another two were destroyed by antiaircraft fire.

Three other Boxer operations were conducted in other parts of the Canal Zone—among them the bombardment of Green Island (Boxer 5)—but these missions were relegated to only thirty to forty sorties each. Their objective was to wear down the Egyptian army with incessant activity, including nocturnal raids.

The five Boxer raids were confined to the length of the Canal Zone and a 2.5- to 4.5-mile-wide strip of land to its west. According to estimates, about one hundred Egyptian soldiers were killed and three hundred wounded. Furthermore, five missile batteries, two radar stations, seventeen artillery batteries, six tank and armored vehicle depots, nineteen outposts, and three bridges were damaged. The IDF also downed twelve Egyptians planes, while losing just two. Nevertheless, these actions did not force the Egyptians to halt their fire.

During the ensuing months, the Air Force took part in the IDF's major operations in other sectors of the Egyptian theater, such as Operation Raviv. When these actions also failed to bring about the desired effect, the Air Force turned to bombardments deep within Egypt. However, these air strikes had limitations of their own. For instance, attacks against stationary targets were not followed up with additional attacks, so that the opportunity to build on the positive momentum was lost. What's more, the destroyed targets—for example, missile batteries or outposts—were usually rebuilt.

Lieutenant Colonel (Res.) Uri Matityahu: The Sayeret Matkal in Operation Bulmus 6. During the Battle of Green Island, Lieutenant Colonel (Res.) Uri Matityahu served as the deputy commander of a team led by Captain Ehud Ram, of blessed memory. When Ehud was killed early on in the battle, Matityahu assumed command. From the moment he arrived at the compound, Uri Matityahu played an active role in the fighting and later took part in the effort to rescue the wounded. Moreover, he was the only member of the Sayeret on the rubber boat that broke down on the way back to Sinai:

> Notwithstanding the outstanding achievements, the debriefings of the Green Island raid, upon which Ze'ev Almog predicated his account, only cover the experiences of one of the parties that participated in that same mission.[13] When I asked Ze'ev why the Sayeret was not involved in the debriefing, he was quite frank: "It took so much time [just] to debrief the twenty people [from the S-13] . . . [In addition], it was like Rashomon. . . ."[14] There is no absolute truth. Every soldier and every commando sees the truth from his own angle. In consequence, it was extremely difficult to correlate the stories and put together an objective picture of what transpired. In essence, it is inevitably impossible to reach an absolute, objective truth; you can only approach it.
>
> For various reasons, the Sayeret Matkal is always running ahead. As is known, the raid took place during the period after the Six Day War,

and the Sayeret was so busy that it had no time for holding debriefings. That said, it's a shame that more of an effort wasn't made to examine the Sayeret's performance during the Green Island raid, for Ze'ev Almog's debriefings managed to put the S-13 "on the map."

The cooperation between the Sayeret Matkal and S-13 was excellent even before Operation Bulmus 6. The mission load in the immediate aftermath of the war mushroomed, for in one fell swoop Israel found itself with brand-new borders, some of which abutted different bodies of water. During the missions, the two units acted in concert and even maintained a rather interesting division of work, which was initiated by Ze'ev Almog and the Sayeret's Uzi Yairi: they taught us how to dive—we completed a scuba course within the framework of the Shayetet—and our combat soldiers taught them how to fight on the ground. Until the raid against Green Island, the Shayetet's personnel were not recognized as combat soldiers by the IDF, and this mission—undoubtedly and indisputably—put them on the map. My colleagues in the Sayeret (myself included) were personally acquainted with every member of the S-13 that participated in the operation at Green Island. From our perspective, working with these truly special people was one of the most incredible experiences we ever had.

When the Sayeret's troops arrived on the roof of the fortress, the face-to-face battle was well under way. By that point, 70 percent of the Shayetet's commandos had run out of ammunition. The troops were operating in an open expanse without cover, and everyone I saw was nursing grenade wounds. Only Gadi Kroll was still capable of functioning, and the man was everywhere. The exemplary conduct of the wounded sent shivers up my spine, and it was particularly moving to see how they evacuated themselves from the battlefield on their own.

Green Island was crushed to smithereens. Fourteen years later—after I had already left the army and had only recently returned to the Sayeret as a deputy division commander—I met up with Ze'ev Almog. At the time, Ze'ev had arranged a cruise (on board a missile boat) to Green Island and all the other sites along the canal where we had seen action. Bereaved families participated in the excursion, and the tour was exceptionally moving. When we reached Green Island, one of the things that astonished me the most was that nothing remained! The entire is-land was in utter ruins as a result of the Air Force's bombardment after the raid. And this was the same fortress that all attempts to damage it and all artillery salvos, failed to bring down its thick walls. Only then did we understand the significance of the 1,000-kg bombs that the IDF planes dropped on the island during the pulverization that was exacted on the compound after the mission.

We were very fortunate to team up with the S-13, in both exercises and operations alike. This group of men from the Shayetet set new stan-dards at Green Island. They were an incredible bunch, and we referred to many of them as "living legends." Their feats during the mission were an expression of their determination, valor, and camaraderie. It is hard to believe that such devotion and sacrifice actually exists. The Shayetet's people were willing to do everything—at almost any cost—to fulfill the mission. Their professionalism, camaraderie, and unstinting adherence to the mission merit the expression "a job well done!"

Captain (Res.) Uzi Livnat: The S-13 in the Assault on Green Island from the Van-tage Point of the Combatant. Captain (Res.) Uzi Livnat took part in every stage of the mission at Green Island, from the breaching of the target until the final evacuation. Like Uri Matityahu, he was also part of the group that was forced to swim over two miles after the exhausting battle. Uzi Livnat also served as the signaler of the mission commander from the moment the latter made it to the roof. What's more, Uzi even participated in the company commanders' course that analyzed the battle (under the guidance of Lieutenant Colonel [Res.] Avraham Zohar, the representative of the IDF's History Department). Uzi later went on to become the commander of the Shayetet:

At the time of the raid, I was a commando in the S-13 and was about to enroll in the IDF commanders' course. During the mission, I fought in the breaching detail before assuming the role of Ze'ev Almog's signaler. I would like to elucidate four points that I have been "lugging" around in my memory of the raid to this very day.

To begin with, I have always had the utmost respect for the senior echelon for having the audacity to approve the assault on Green Island. That said, my most vivid memory from that period is of the warning that the IDF commander in chief gave to the force's commander, during the final briefing before the mission, to retreat if there were over ten mortal injuries. Only then did I, as a combat soldier, come to the realization that we were heading off on an extremely dangerous mission. Until that very moment, I was under the impression that it was just another mission, like the others I had already been on (for example, the operation at Adabiyah, which relatively speaking was a rather simple operation). It turned out that the Green Island raid was a completely different kettle of fish.

The preparations for the mission form the second topic that bears emphasis. Ze'ev Almog did not mention this issue in his presentation, and justifiably so, for he spoke about the operation from the historical perspective of a researcher. Nevertheless, it is important to note that when we began training for the operation, there was a considerable gap between the necessary and existing skill levels in practically every field. There were many mishaps and problems over the course of the preparations and exercises. These early hardships were enough to shock the people standing on the side as well as those in the thick of things, but they were solved and we proceeded with the operation.

In many respects, both the SOP and the raid itself constituted a whole new world for the Shayetet. For instance, the entire field of the dived assault originated at Green Island. Many years later, the S-13 reached extraordinary levels of proficiency in this sort of raid by virtue of its illustrious start. Ze'ev Almog deserves a large share of the credit for the fact that "we did it."

Third, I wish to discuss the issue of intelligence. As a member of the breaching detail, I was among the twenty men that infiltrated the island and crawled under the bridge. There were aluminum cans scattered all over the ground and we couldn't help but make noise. I was terrified that the guards would hear us. It was extremely difficult to position twenty people in that narrow space beneath the bridge. There was a sense that the moment we exited its shadows, the Egyptians would spot us. We knew that there was an opening in the gate, but were barred from reaching it. Although the breaching detail wanted to spread out and protect its flanks, this was out of the question so long as one member of the team was busy cutting the fence and the other two were holding the metal rope with flannelette.[15] Moreover, it was quite obvious that if we would have to detonate the Bangalore charge, the entire breaching detail would be doomed. Therefore, we had to continue cutting the fence. I remember myself lying on the fence, unable to fathom how we were supposed to keep quiet while cutting through barbed wire. I thought it would never end. The entire situation seemed beyond the realm of possibility—but this was the plan.

Ilan Egozi was the one who decided to open fire because he thought that the Egyptian guard had spotted us. At that very same moment, a grenade was thrown and Gadi Kroll, who was a few meters behind us, silently passed back the word to all the men to run through the existing breach—not from the spot we had been plugging away at all this time— the instant a bullet was fired.

Notwithstanding the plans, the course of events naturally unfolded in their [sic] own way during the battle itself. We reached the point where people did what had to be done according to the circumstances in the field. For instance, the roof area was nearly as bright as day throughout most of the battle on account of the strong illumination flares that were fired from the enemy's 130-mm guns. Therefore, we were rather exposed, and our tracers seemed to be extraneous. If a sniper had been sitting on gun positions #5 or 6, he would have killed everyone that was on the roof. Therefore, we were very fortunate that the mission ended with six fallen comrades. Had the Egyptians countered in a persistent and discriminating manner, the mission could very well have ended in great tragedy. In practice, our troops maintained a continuity of fire, fought courageously, and displayed professionalism. These are apparently the factors that prevented the Egyptians from doing what they could have.

The fourth and final topic I would like to discuss is the ability and willingness to draw conclusions. From a physical standpoint, the Shayetet finished the battle battered and bruised, but displayed the wherewithal to embark on a brand-new course. The desire to learn from the battle transformed the way the unit was run; expedited the pace at which it progressed in the coming years; and preserved the Shayetet's unique fighting spirit. These virtues were not only passed on to the Shayetet's next generations, but were channeled through the Shayetet to the rest of the Navy's units. The main impetus behind this enterprise was Ze'ev Almog, who subsequently served as the commander of the Red Sea Arena before going on to become the admiral of the Navy. Many concepts that were forged during the SOP before the assault on Green Island—how to truly run and plan a battle, how to construct a force, and how to prepare equipment—constitute indispensable assets in the Shayetet's arsenal to this very day.

The Green Island raid was a formative event in the annals of the Shayetet. Three of its participants reached the rank of rear admiral and went on to command the Navy. In my opinion, they reached these heights solely on account of this operation. In addition, four other participants reached the rank of captain in the Navy and another two reached the rank of commander. The Shayetet's people believed in the need, ability, fitness, and potential of the unit to execute this sort of operation, and they proved that they were right.

THREE

Operation Escort

The Sinking of Torpedo Boats in the Gulf of Suez

In early August 1969, the General Staff decided to launch Operation Raviv (rain), an armored assault along the west coast of the Gulf of Suez. The force would be transported to the Egyptian coast on Navy landing crafts.

Before this decision came to fruition, there were plans to conduct another armored assault, Operation Balash (detective) immediately following the Green Island raid. Two days before the latter, on the night of July 17–18, a team of defensive divers from Unit 707 of the Navy conducted an advance survey (Operation Balash Katan, small detective) of a landing beach that was slated for the Armored Corps' offensive. However, the beach was found to be unfit for the mission at hand, and a new location was needed.

On account of the Green Island raid, the Egyptians reinforced the northern Gulf of Suez with two P-183 torpedo boats, which were transferred from Hurgada in the northern Red Sea. The boats subsequently patrolled the stretch of water between Ras Adabiyah and the fuel terminal at Ras Sadat on a regular basis and occasionally continued southward to Marsa T'lmat. The Egyptian torpedoes constituted a formidable obstacle to the IDF's ability to launch Operation Raviv. In fact, the armored assault would not be possible unless the torpedo boats were sunk and a replacement landing beach was found. These conditions thus formed the backdrop for Operation Escort, in which the S-13 was charged with conducting a clandestine patrol for the purpose of locating a suitable beach. The results of this mission would determine the fate of the armored raid.

The Egyptian torpedo boats did not maintain a set patrolling or berthing routine. We estimated that they would drop anchor during the night somewhere within a 2.5-mile-wide swath of sea between Ras Sadat's fuel terminal and the *Evangelos*, a sunken Greek ship. Yet, given the uncertainties involved, it was not going to be easy finding the torpedo boats at their anchorage sites.

The General Staff also considered assigning the task to the Air Force, but the option was ruled out due to the difficulties of locating and identifying the targets with absolute certainty from the air, at night. What's more, an aerial fusillade was likely to be a noisy undertaking that would set off alarm bells throughout the region. This sort of attack was liable to disrupt the landing and ground assault phase of the operation and ruin the chances of catching the enemy off guard. On the other hand, a daylight aerial strike was precluded on the assumption that the torpedo boats would be located in areas that were protected by missile or antiaircraft batteries during the day.

In consequence, the S-13's divers and their seaworthy pigs were deemed to be the right team for the job. The surreptitious operation was designed to allow the armored force to land on the heels of the sinking. With this in mind, it was decided to reconnoiter a site that was located to the west of Ras Sudr for the purpose of determining whether it was suitable for the mission at hand.

Operation Raviv Katan

On August 13, 1969, about three weeks after the raid on Green Island, a Shayetet force set out to survey a landing beach on the west coast of the Gulf of Suez. A team of two pigs and four swimmers, all under the command of Lieutenant Commander Emanuel Paz ("Paulin"), was towed from Ras Sudr by a pair of Bertrams. After eight miles, the pigs headed off toward the Egyptian coast, while the Bertrams returned to the middle of the Gulf and waited for the commandos to complete the mission.

Concurrently, the enemy torpedo boats were in the middle of a patrol from Ras Sadat to Marsa T'lmet and back. The routes taken by the Israeli and Egyptian forces—not the forces themselves—actually crisscrossed, but the torpedo boats continued along their way without showing any signs of having detected our presence. Upon discovering that the torpedo boats were on the move, the Bertrams edged closer to the Israeli shore. Meanwhile, the pig force proceeded according to plan and completed the survey, without leaving any traces.

Several critical discoveries were made over the course of the patrol. Not only was the beach found to be appropriate for an armed landing, but the patrol's contribution went beyond the scope of the landing operation, as it basically served as a "live model" for the sinking action and important data was secured about the enemy's patterns of behavior. Once again, the pigs proved their operational advantage in the field of the surreptitious entry, and their transport by means of Bertrams also proved to be efficacious. Since the distance covered on Operation Raviv Katan was similar to that of the planned sinking action, inferences could be drawn from the former about Escort. The mission also enabled us to put our techno-logistical methods for reaching Ras Sudr to the full test. Similarly, we examined several possibilities for dropping the pigs into the water at locations that were well beyond the enemy's sights. The route that was ultimately chosen allowed us to circumvent the entire vicinity of the Suez Canal, where the Egyptians were more likely to expose our intentions and the troops were susceptible to shelling and mines.

During the patrol, the torpedo boats were spotted thirteen miles from Ras Sudr and five miles north of the pigs' traversal route. These distances were within range of our radars, and this turned out to be instrumental in our plans to sink the boats. Furthermore, the findings made it abundantly clear that the torpedo boats were liable to be in motion during the operation, and not at rest.

The only significant difference between the survey of the landing beach and the sinking operation was the phase of the lunar cycle. The full moon on the night of the patrol impeded our efforts to some extent, as the pigs had to keep their distance from the shore in order to avoid being detected. Consequently, the commandos could not actually identify the beach and were assisted by an electronic guidance system. On the other hand, the lack of a full moon on the designated night of the attack constituted a major hindrance, for we were charged with locating and physically identifying the "slippery" targets.

On August 21, the Operations Directorate informed us that Operation Escort would be carried out on September 5–6 (it was eventually delayed to September 7–8). In addition, I was invited to present the operation plan for the approval of Commander-in-Chief Haim Bar-Lev the very next day.

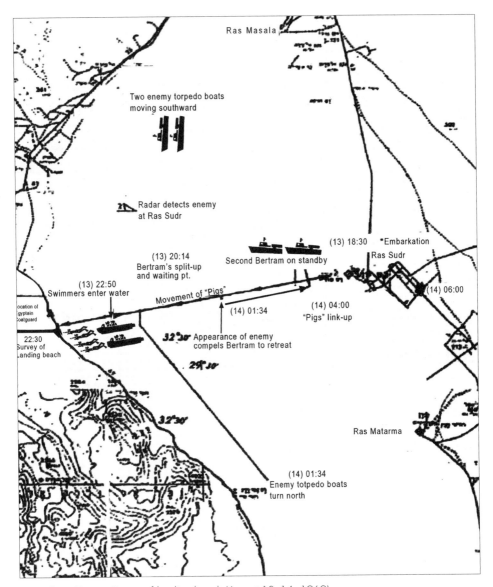

Ras Masala

Two enemy torpedo boats
moving southward

Radar detects enemy
at Ras Sudr

(13) 18:30 ▪Embarkation
Ras Sudr

(13) 20:14
Bertram's split-up
and waiting pt.

Second Bertram on standby

(13) 22:50
Swimmers enter water

(14) 06:00

location of
gyptain
coatguard

Movement of "Pigs"

(14) 04:00
"Pigs" link-up

(14) 01:34

22:30
Survey of
Landing beach

Appearance of enemy
compels Bertram to retreat

Ras Matarma

(14) 01:34
Enemy totpedo boats
turn north

Raviv Katan—Survey of landing beach (August 13–14, 1969).

Operation Escort

Operation Escort was a classic naval commando operation: the sinking of
military seafaring vessels by divers, in the northern Gulf of Suez, within the
framework of the War of Attrition. This was the first successful operation of
its kind in the annals of the IDF.

Several characteristics set Operation Escort apart from the rest. This was the S-13's third large raid within a space of two and a half months. The mission set new, unprecedented standards and transcended the present borders in all that concerned the means, methods, and durability of the equipment used, as well as the level of physical execution required of the combatants. Operation Escort indeed broke the IDF's existing "operational mold" by destroying targets that were active maritime vessels in the Egyptian zone of combat. The operation constituted a preliminary phase and prerequisite for an armored landing and assault on a sixty-two-mile, Egyptian strip of coast. The Navy and Air Force also played instrumental roles in the subsequent offensive.

On account of its unique characteristics, Operation Escort constitutes, along with the raids at Adabiyah and Green Island, one of the S-13's three prototype operations in the maritime and coastal theater. These operations continue to serve as model operations for the Israeli Navy Commando. The three operations were carried out in succession, and the distinct infiltration method that was employed in each specific mission had a decisive impact on their success:

- At Adabiyah, the S-13 struck a defended coastal structure and the fighting was conducted in a built-up area. The target was infiltrated by a force of swimmers.
- The Green Island raid was an attack against an armed fortress in the middle of the sea. The battle was waged in a built-up, crammed, and complicated area, which was infiltrated by a force of divers.
- Operation Escort was carried out by frogmen who were transported to an uncertain target on board pigs. Upon getting within striking range, the commandos dove to the boats and sunk them with limpet mines.

FORMING UP

On August 22, the day we were scheduled to present the operation plan to the General Staff, I received an unexpected call from Bar-Lev to meet him in his office for a private discussion. "There is no need to present me the details of the plan," he told me at the meeting. "For you guys, this is like having bread and butter for breakfast. I called you in to stress the fact that the execu-

"Pigs."

Egyptian P-183 torpedo boat, made in the USSR.

tion of Operation Raviv is riding on the success of Escort. There won't be a Raviv unless you sink those torpedo boats!"

I was already cognizant of Operation Raviv's dependence on Escort, but Bar-Lev's words further underscored the responsibility that was thrust on our shoulders, namely the very fate of Raviv. I brooded over whether the commander in chief's statement about "bread and butter for breakfast" was indicative of an egregious underestimation of the incredible level of difficulty —operational, human, and technical—that this sort of mission demanded, or whether it was merely Bar-Lev's way of expressing his confidence that we would once again make every effort to justify his deep faith in us. From the letter of commendation that I received from Bar-Lev after the mission, it was obvious that he had been well aware of the difficulties involved and wanted us to prove that his confidence in the unit was warranted.

Operation Escort was the first mission that the high command assigned directly to the Shayetet. The operation was an integral part of a large campaign, as the mission's success was a precondition for the launching of another operation. The sense of duty, along with the professional opportunity and challenge of carrying out a classic sinking action by frogmen, spurred us on to do our very best.

With respect to the inner needs of the S-13, I considered the retention of the unit's fighting momentum and continuity of its operational activity to be of utmost importance in the aftermath of the Green Island raid, especially due to the loss of three outstanding *lochamim* (warriors) and the incapacitation (mainly temporary) of eleven others due to injury. Any prolonged stoppage in the unit's operational activity ran the risk of deflating the fighting spirit that had taken hold of the Shayetet. Therefore, I felt that we had no right to slow down and lick our wounds.

At the end of our meeting, I had but one request for the commander in chief: to launch Operation Escort no later than August 28 (*Elul* 14),[1] the day before the moon begins to wane, even though such an ambitious deadline would have subjected the unit to intense time pressure. Given the torpedo boats' low profile (flat build), the lack of advanced knowledge as to their place of anchorage, the large swath of sea (about 2.5 miles) that the operators would have to comb, and the lack of a pier or some other point of reference by which to navigate, the moonlight would improve our chances of locating and identifying the targets. However, our needs clashed with the commander in chief's plans to transfer the tank carriers from Sharm al-Sheikh under the cover of the next batch of dark nights (beginning September 5), for the purpose of concealing the IDF's intentions. Consequently, the dates of Operation Raviv and Operation Escort were pushed ahead, and we would have to contend with poor visibility during the mission. There were, however, advantages to the postponement, as the extra time would allow us to solve some of the more complex problems that we faced and work out the kinks in the plans that had already been adopted.

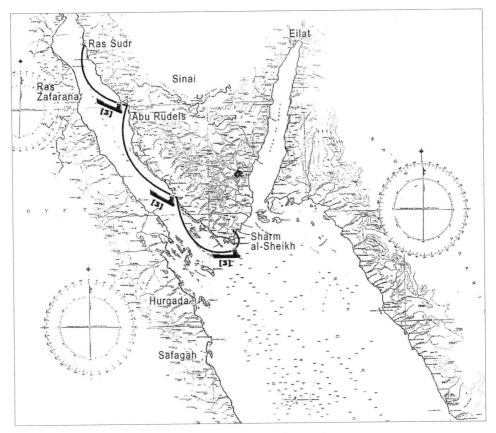

LCTs proceed from Sharm al-Sheikh to Ras Sudr over three nights.

STAFFING THE FORCES

Despite the casualties that were incurred during the raid on Green Island, there were enough candidates within the Shayetet's combat strength to forge the requisite team of nine skilled commandos in operational form: four pig operators, four "foot" divers, and one "pigist" in reserve. Certain guidelines were established for selecting the most appropriate men for this unique assignment:

- A high level of professionalism.
- Every effort would be made to include relatively fresh combat troops in the force.
- An opportunity would be given to officers whose operational activity was relatively limited during the previous year (primarily due to the fact that

they were outside the unit's framework at the time), so that they could acquire some first-rate operational and professional experience.

In light of these criteria, most of the soldiers that were assigned key roles in Operation Escort did not actively participate in the fighting on Green Island, but served in auxiliary roles (for example, members of the holding and diversionary detail and rubber craft operators) or were outside the regular framework of the Shayetet's operations during this period. Operation Escort also presented me with an opportunity to expand the circle of the unit's future command echelons and base their leadership and authority on full-fledged combat experience.

Two of the men who met the criteria, Lieutenant Rafi Miloh and First Lieutenant Shlomo Eshel, requested to join the force, while I asked a third, Chief Petty Officer Oded Nir, to come on board. Rafi, an outstanding frogman commander, was on sabbatical without pay, and Shlomo, a talented officer in the pig unit, declared even before the mission that he intended on returning to the unit within the framework of the standing army.[2] Oded, a superb *lochem*, who specialized in all the Shayetet's combat professions—foot diver, pigist, explosive boats—served as a rubber craft operator in the Green Island raid. After the mission, he was sent to complete his matriculation studies,[3] so that he could eventually become a munitions officer. Additionally, Oded was on my boat at the entrance to Port Said during the Six Day War, and I was impressed by his technical prowess and grace under pressure.

One of the exceptions was Ami Ayalon, who played a leading role in Green Island. Ami, a future candidate for commander of the pig unit, was recovering from the wounds he suffered on Green Island, but insisted on participating in Operation Escort. The unit's doctor, Shimon Slavin, who tended to Ami, determined that he was fit for the mission and I thus included him on the roster. All the other candidates—Aryeh Yitzchak ("Aryo"), Eldad Dinur ("Fatty"), Shlomo Asif ("Bigler"), Avishai Ben-Yosef, and Shmuel Tamir— were outstanding pigists in the regular service who had participated in most of the Shayetet's operations in the north of the gulf during the past year, primarily as pig operators.

GUARANTEEING THE ELEMENT OF SURPRISE

All the planning considerations were naturally subjugated to fulfilling the mission itself—the sinking action—and to taking the enemy by surprise, both of which were prerequisites for carrying out the armored landing and assault. Consequently, precautions against revealing the IDF's intentions were a major emphasis of our preparations.

On account of the many operations that we had already conducted in the northern gulf, Egypt's attention was focused on the coastal debarkation point at Ras Masala. For example, the heavy bombardment that the Egyptians exacted on Ras Masala following the raids on Adabiyah and Green Island constitutes firm evidence that the venue was in their sights. As a result, we decided to embark from Ras Sudr instead of Ras Masala, even though this would markedly increase the distance to the target. Likewise, we planned to reach Ras Sudr via a long and roundabout route in order to hide our intentions. After saddling the pigs onto "rocking cradles," the pieces would be transported from Atlit, in northern Israel, down to Eilat in a closed semitrailer truck. From Eilat, they would be freighted by sea (on board a landing craft) to Sharm al-Sheikh, whereupon they would return to solid ground and make their way to Ras Sudr on the road that spans the length of the Gulf of Suez. As mentioned, this grueling techno-logistical enterprise had already proven its mettle in Operation Raviv Katan.

With respect to the operation itself, the two pigs would not regroup once the mines had been planted on the targets. Although linking them up was advantageous from a safety standpoint, it would force us to operate the wireless communications, which was liable to disclose their location and reveal our intentions to the enemy. In this particular instance, the need to maintain strict wireless silence trumped safety considerations.

The range of a pig was roughly forty miles, which was less than the distance to the target and back (about forty-five miles). This statistic did not leave an adequate or safe enough amount of electricity reserves in the pig's accumulators. Consequently, Bertram patrol boats, which were stationed at the IDF naval base at Ras Sudr, would be used to tow the pigs within striking distance of the zone of operation. Since Bertrams could be picked up by enemy radar from considerable distances, they could only shuttle the pigs eight miles from Ras Sudr. This same method was used during the earlier recon patrol of the landing beach (Raviv Katan) and thus served as a model for the sinking action. In any event, this arrangement afforded the operators a certain degree of comfort, as they would be able stay dry and preserve their strength by lounging on board the decks of the Bertrams throughout the towage phase.

As already noted, our efforts to locate the targets were hindered by the following factors: the lack of moonlight on the scheduled night of the mission; the low profile of the Egyptian torpedo boats; the lack of information concerning the time and place of the boats' berthing; and the extensive area (2.5 nautical miles) that the force would have to comb. Correspondingly, it was incumbent upon the commandos to maintain an absolute veil of secrecy during both the hunt and mine-planting phases, so as to avoid arousing the enemy's suspicion. For the sake of contending with these problems, the route to the targets was divided into five intervals. At each leg of the journey, the movement formation, placement of pieces, and navigation would change in accordance with the prevailing conditions in the force's present location and the presumed location of the torpedo boats. Once the pigs parted ways with the Bertrams, their movement would be specifically adapted to the risk of exposure and proximity to the targets at each particular section. Similarly, their navigation means would correspond with their movement formation and degree of submergence.

There were five phases of Operation Escort. During the first leg of the journey, the Bertrams were supposed to tow the pigs above the surface to a point approximately eight miles from Ras Sudr. The navigation was to be handled by the Bertram crews. At the eight-mile mark, the pigs would part ways with the surface vessels and continue above the surface as an independent pair with the help of an electronic guidance system. They were slated to reach the staging area, a mile or two from the fuel terminal. Upon reaching the staging area, the pigs were instructed to enter minimal buoyancy mode (a position in which the pig is submerged and only the soldiers' heads are above the surface). The pigs would then split up and proceed to their own combing areas, where they would start hunting for the torpedo boats. Both areas were in the vicinity of the fuel terminal and the adjacent discharging tanker, which constituted prominent objects that could readily be used as points of reference for orientation and navigation. In the event that the torpedo boats were not found in this swath of sea, the pigs would move to the next section.

The search during the fourth phase was to be conducted beneath the surface. Until the targets were located, the pig would occasionally ascend and the respective commanders would sneak a peek in order to set a course. Each vessel would comb its predetermined side of the zone, to the east or west of the discharging tanker. Once the berthed torpedo boats were spotted, the pig that made the discovery would land on the nearby seabed. The pair of foot divers would then exit the pig and fasten the limpet mines on the targets. The two operators would wait on board the parked vehicle until the divers returned.

The depth, currents, and transparency of the water in the zone of operation obligated the pig to touch down on the seafloor near, albeit not directly beneath, the torpedo boats. In addition to the pig operators, the sea state also necessitated the services of a pair of foot divers in each pig

According to the maps, the charted seabed in the targets' vicinity was as much as forty-six feet deep. At these depths, it is forbidden to stay beneath the surface with combat oxygen rebreather sets for too long due to the danger of oxygen toxicity. Open-circuit breathing sets solved the poisoning problem, but these devices spout "revealing" bubbles. Therefore, the decision was made to use the latter, which were built into the pig, for extended stays beneath the surface at depths of greater than thirty-three feet. As such, the divers would use open-circuit devices while waiting on the seabed for the divers to return, and the latter would switch to the bubble-free, closed-circuit, oxygen-nourished combat devices (rebreathers) before ascending to the targets.

As noted, the clear waters of the Red Sea forced the operators to dock the pigs on the seabed at a moderate distance from the torpedo boats, so that Egyptian sailors on deck would not detect the vehicle. The landing was also intended to prevent the pig from being swept away by the expected currents in the area. After touching down on the seabed, the foot divers would exit the craft, but their bodies would be tethered to the vehicle by means of a recoiling tape line, so that they could find their way back to the pigs after planting the mines.

PLANTING THE MINES

The hull of the enemy's P-183 torpedo boat was made of wood, but the bottom was plated with metal (aluminum or bronze). It was incumbent upon us to do everything in our power to avoid the less than far-fetched scenario in which the force would complete the long and arduous journey to the targets, only

"Foot" divers debark from a "pig" that has landed on the seabed.

to run into problems with the limpet mines. With this in mind, the Shayetet developed three separate planting techniques:

- Fastening the device by means of magnets that were snapped on to the base of the mine. If the bottom of the boats were plated with aluminum or brass, the magnets would not stick.
- Connecting rubber bands to the limpet, so that it could be tied around the propeller axes.
- Planting the mine to the bottom of the boat with the help of a mechanical screw. However, if the metal was too strong or the wood was rotted, the screw was liable to slip out.

The divers would choose the most appropriate technique upon reaching the boat and evaluating the conditions at hand. Even so, none of the techniques could fully guarantee the attachment of the anti-removal system, which was developed by the Israel Military Industries and the Shayetet. These mechanisms cause the mine to go off if it begins to fall off the surface. In Operation Escort, the non-removal apparatus was critical because there was a decent chance that the torpedo boats would start moving before the limpet's delay mechanism expired; in the absence of a functioning anti-removal system, the mines would fall off and the enemy boats would unwittingly skirt

disaster. In order to overcome this stumbling block, we adopted the following measures during the SOP. The Shayetet's demolition officer, Lieutenant Israel Roth presided over the development of a pyrotechnic screw. A propellant charge was installed in the head of a mechanical fastening screw and activated by pulling a safety catch. The charge was designed to thrust the screw deep into the bottom of the boat and was even powerful enough to enable the screw to penetrate a layer of metal.

During a "live" experiment conducted at sea, the pyrotechnic screw was inserted into the bottom of a boat with a wooden hull—the T-204, a decommissioned Israeli torpedo boat. The objective of the maneuver was to determine whether the propellant's subaqueous blast could be heard from within the boat. In an ensuing "model" drill before the mission, the T-204 simulated the enemy and had live mines set off on its underside.

Forces and Assignments

Four forces were set up to execute the mission or provide assistance:

FORCE AND ALIGNMENT	ASSIGNMENT	COMMENTS
Force I: • 2 pigs • 4 operators + 4 foot divers	• Transport the divers • Destroy the torpedo boats	Two mines per diver
Force II: • 2 Bertrams • 2 rubber crafts + 8 soldiers	• Tow the pigs and provide support • Poised to offer assistance and rescue the attack force	
Force III: • Super Frelon helicopter • Nord planes • Fighter jets • Electronic Guidance System	• Rescue alert • Communication relay • Defense, offense • Direct the naval force	Stationed at Ras Sudr On standby of 30 minutes Stationed at Ras Sudr
Force IV: • Southern Command— 122-mm artillery battery	• On standby to shell Adabiyah	

If the torpedo boats were on the move during the first night, another attempt would be made the next night. The first night was thus defined as a "violent patrol": it would stay within the framework of a mere patrol if the mandatory conditions for an attack did not present themselves; and it would turn "violent," if these conditions did exist, namely the boats were found to be berthing.

The Final Plan

According to the final plan, which evolved over the course of the SOP, the entire maritime force—the pigs, Bertram boats (charged with towing the former), and accompanying rubber crafts—would set out in concert from Ras Sudr toward Ras Sadat, with the help of an electronic guidance system. After advancing eight miles, the pig operators and divers would transfer from the Bertrams to the pigs and continue on their own, above the surface and under the direction of the guidance system, to the staging area (one to two miles from the terminal); the Bertram boats would backtrack a bit and position themselves in their designated standby point; and the rubber crafts would head eastward to their own standby position off the coast of Ras Daheisha.

Upon reaching their staging area, the pigs would switch to minimal buoyancy mode, shut off the electronic guidance system, and begin the hunt for the torpedo boats in the vicinity of the discharging tanker at Ras Sadat's fuel terminal. If the boats were located, the pigs would land on the seafloor and engage the enemy targets. In the event that the boats were not found in this zone, the pigs would submerge and enter the next section, which was adjacent to the first and extended to the sunken Greek ship, the *Evangelos*, 2.5 miles to the south. This area would be scanned by means of occasional surface peeks. Under the command of Lieutenant Rafi Miloh, the team in pig #3 (also consisting of First Lieutenant Shlomo Eshel, the pig commander, Chief Petty Officer Oded Nir, and Petty Officer First Class Shmuel Tamir[4]) would comb the area to the west of the tanker. Correspondingly, the force in pig #4, headed by First Lieutenant Ami Ayalon (alongside Chief Petty Officer Eldad Dinur, the pig commander, Petty Officer First Class Shlomo Asif, and Petty Officer First Class Avishai Ben-Yosef) would comb the area to the east. After planting the mines and activating the mechanisms, each pig would return on its own to Ras Sudr.

Execution

Everything went according to plan until the force reached the staging area and the Bertrams and rubber crafts departed. As the pigs dipped into minimal buoyancy mode, the Egyptian torpedo boats suddenly appeared and closed in on them at full throttle. The pigs executed an "emergency dive" and bided time on the seafloor. As the torpedo boats passed over them, the eight commandos heard blasts of gunfire and explosives. Sometime later, the pigs proceeded with the plans. The vehicles headed off, independently and beneath the surface, to comb their routes in search of the berthed torpedo boats, by means of frequent surface peeks. However, the targets were not found in the presumed area, so the crews moved on to the next zone near the *Evangelos*, where they operated from 0215 to 0300, but the targets were nowhere to be found. The pigs thus received an order at 0307 to return to Ras Sudr, and the command post decided to resume the hunt the following Sunday.

The sight of the Egyptian torpedo boats plowing straight toward the pigs and discharging rounds in their direction seemed to indicate that the force had been detected or, at the very least, aroused the enemy's suspicions. If the Egyptians indeed thought that something was up, they were liable to keep the torpedo boats on the move and avoid dropping anchor. In consequence, it was imperative for us to ratchet up the level of surreptitiousness and let the enemy troops in the area "calm down." Moreover, we needed a time-out to recharge the pigs' electric accumulators. In this light, a decision was made to defer the next attempt to execute the demolition to the night of September 7–8.

Within the framework of our preparations for the "repeat performance," a series of changes were introduced. This included pushing up the mission's departure by one hour (to 1700), for the following reasons:

- The desire to put a fair amount of sea behind us during daylight, when the Egyptians usually refrained from operating their radars.
- An earlier arrival to the designated combing zones would improve our chances of "catching" the torpedo boats before they left their anchorage site and increase the hours of darkness at our disposal for hunting down the targets.

Similar to the first night (Escort 1), the split-up was to take place at a distance of eight miles from Ras Sudr (but this time, at an earlier hour: 1845), and the Bertram boats and rubber crafts would return to the vicinity of Ras Sudr, where they would wait out at sea for the pigs to complete the mission. The revised plan also called for reducing the pigs' stay above the surface. Upon reaching within three miles of the target, the approach would be carried out in minimal buoyancy, without the assistance of the electronic guidance system. This mode of movement was likely to be quite arduous, as the pigs would be forced to advance straight into the oncoming waves and against the prevailing winds. Nevertheless, the crews could draw on the lessons from the night of the first action. For instance, their familiarity with the terrain and targets would minimize navigation problems. Likewise, the two pigs would part ways about 1,000 yards east of the discharging tanker at the fuel terminal. In addition, the combing to the south would essentially be conducted beneath the surface, as only the pig commander would occasionally stick his head above water in order to steal a glance and direct the vehicle toward the targets.

Operation Escort 2 was carried out a mere two days after Escort 1. Each assignment entailed eleven consecutive hours in the water over the course of a journey covering a total of forty-five miles. This feat exacted a grueling physical and mental toll on the commandos. What's more, the conditions during the second night were destined to become even more daunting.

This time around I reinstated Aryeh Yitzchak to the team, and Shmuel Tamir reassumed his reserve role. The operation got under way at 1610, when the pigs were lowered into the water with the help of the technical staff, which carried out the "zero-in balance" procedure.[5] Correspondingly, the combat team held a "soldiers' chat" with the commander in chief, who reemphasized the fact that the sinking of the torpedo boats was a prerequisite for the launching of Operation Raviv.

At 1710, the pigs were hitched onto the Bertram boats, and the "pigs," Bertrams, and rubber crafts headed out. The force reached the designated split-up point eight miles from Ras Sudr in about an hour and a half (at 1845 and seventy-five minutes earlier than the first night), whereupon the pigs detached from the Bertrams and the divers entered their vehicles. The surface crafts then returned to the vicinity of Ras Sudr, where they waited at sea. Thirty minutes after the forces parted ways, the electronic guidance system was shut down, but the detection conditions proved to be quite favorable. It turned out that the dry spell that had swept over the region created atmospheric conditions which caused electromagnetic waves—for instance, radar and wireless communication signals—to disperse well beyond the range that we were accustomed to. Consequently, we would be able to continue keeping track of the pigs on the radar and adjust their route, should the need arise.

At 1945, the pigs were eleven miles from Ras Sudr, yet we could still see them on the radar screen. However, this meant that if the Egyptians, who were only nine miles from the pigs, switched on their radar, they would in all likelihood detect them at once. For the sake of preventing the Egyptians from discovering the force and thereby foiling the entire operation (including the armored assault), I felt compelled to make an unprecedented and heart-wrenching decision: to have the pigs descend into minimal buoyancy right there and then. As a pigist myself, I knew that I was practically asking the soldiers to do the impossible—to advance 9 nautical miles with only their heads above water, while the northerly waves continuously smacked them square in the face. However, this was a necessary step, for it was the only way to keep the torpedo boats from going into motion. I thus relayed the troops a single code word instructing them to enter minimal buoyancy at once, and the pigs thus instantly disappeared from the radar screen.[6]

At 2140, the pigs reached the staging area, which was 1,100 yards west of the discharging tanker. The entire combat force, as well as the detail in pig #3, was under the command of Rafi Miloh, while Ami Ayalon presided over the detail in pig #4. Upon receiving Rafi's order, the two pigs split up, submerged, and proceeded to their designated zones: pig #3 covered the area to the west of the tanker, under the direction of the vehicle's commander, Shlomo Eshel; and pig #4, commanded by the pigist Eldad Dinur ("Fatty"), handled the eastern zone. Both teams conducted the search by means of intermittent surface peeks.

Some twenty-five minutes later (at 2320 and about an hour and fifteen minutes after leaving the staging area), Fatty noticed a dark mass near the *Evangelos* and directed the pig in that direction. Soon after, Fatty positively identified the two torpedo boats standing next to each other and tied to a buoy. He landed the vehicle on the seabed—thirty-six feet beneath the surface at a safe distance from the targets—from where the crew could hear the generators of the torpedo boats. Fatty then signaled to Ami and Avishai to exit the pig and dive westward. The two frogmen, who were attached to the

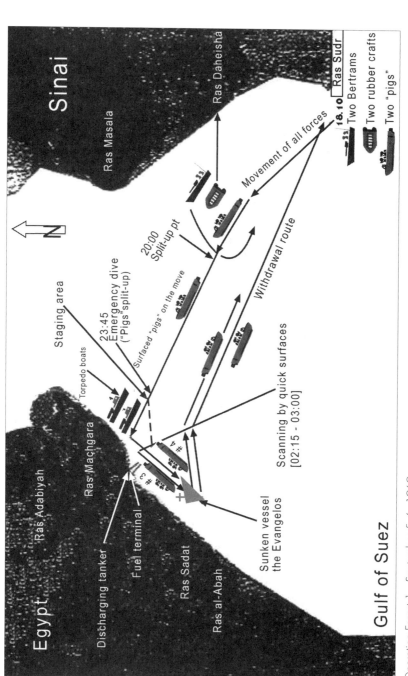

Operation Escort 1—September 5-6, 1969.

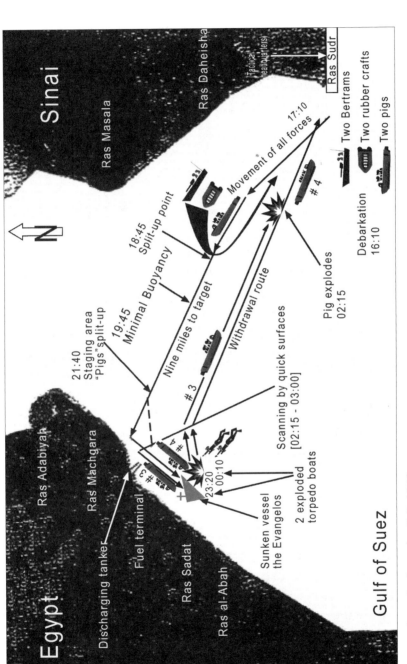

Operation Escort 2—September 7–8, 1969.

pig by tape lines, moved "on foot" toward the targets, while Fatty and his co-operator Bigler waited in the vehicle for the divers to return.

Ami and Avishai rose to the surface in order to confirm the identification and record the route to the boats on their compass. They then re-submerged and advanced at a depth of twenty feet until they were directly beneath the targets, whereupon they ascended to the underside of the first boat and began the task of planting the mines.

The first limpet mine's pyrotechnic screw didn't work, so Ami and Avishai attached the mine onto the boat's axis with the help of magnets. Fearing that the device might slip off, the two frogmen decided not to activate its anti-removal system. They then fastened the second limpet closer to the bow with the help of the screw and activated the mine. However, they once again passed up on the anti-removal system, for they noticed that there was too much space between the base of the mine and the boat's surface. This gap was liable to cause the anti-removal system to go off when the divers removed the limpet's safety pin.

At the second boat, the first mine did not stick onto the bottom, so Ami and Avishai used magnets to fasten it to the axis, which again precluded the activation of the anti-removal system. The fourth mine firmly clasped on to the bottom, thereby enabling them to finally activate at least one of the anti-removal systems. Ami and Avishai then returned to the pig via one of the tape lines, while cutting the second cord in order to avoid getting entangled.

Twenty minutes after Fatty's initial identification of the torpedo boats (at 2340), pig #4 detached from the seabed and headed east for fifteen minutes, in order to distance itself from the targets. At 2355, we received the crew's coded report: "Axe on two dogs; in the right dog, the seed is liable to fall!" In other words, the mines have been fastened on both torpedo boats, but one of the mines on the boat to the right has an anti-removal system that is liable to fall off. This report, which was sent to the command post, was also meant to pass on the location of the targets to the second pig, which had obviously yet to find the targets. Ami also wanted to inform the second crew that the planted mines did not satisfactorily "cover" the two boats, as only one of the mines—the one with the activated anti-removal system—was certain to go off. Finally, Ami's message warned the next pair of divers to avoid knocking off the mine that contained the activated anti-removal system. I passed on the message to the men in pig #3 via the command post and signaled them the location of the targets vis à vis the *Evangelos*.

Shlomo Eshel, the pig commander of the second vehicle, realized that he was close to the targets. Within minutes, he located the torpedo boats, dove beneath them, and landed on the seabed nearby. Shlomo and Aryeh Yitzchak ("Aryo") remained on the pig as the divers, Rafi Miloh and Oded Nir, advanced "on foot," while hugging the seabed, until they were underneath the targets. At this point, they identified the mines, stood on the seabed, and dove up to the bottom of the boat in order to plant the limpets. The two frogmen managed to fasten all the mines they were carrying onto the section of the underlying surface closest to the bow, in front of the mines that were planted by their predecessors. Since the traction of the surface was firm and pliant, they managed to operate the anti-removal systems in all four mines and thus guaranteed the destruction of the torpedo boats.

These Egyptian torpedo boats were the first enemy naval vessels to be mined with limpets in an active IDF combat zone with the help of pigs.[7] This sort of mission constitutes a high point in the life of the frogman, who dedicates years of hard training to just this sort of assignment.

On September 8, at 0010, after putting about twenty minutes between themselves and the targets, pig #3 reported that all four mines had been planted and each of the attendant anti-removal systems had been activated. Upon hearing the news, the crew on board pig #4 offered its congratulations. Pig #3 then continued to Ras Sudr, while maintaining wireless silence. At 0200, a "control signal" (a single code word) came in from the two pigs notifying us that all was well and they were heading back to base, as planned.

Fifteen minutes later, the men on pig #4 heard an explosion not far behind them and attempted to make contact with pig #3, but there was no response. Nevertheless, it seemed far-fetched to tie the blast to pig #3 and they assumed the torpedo boats had exploded. Although the delay mechanism was set for four to six hours and only two hours had passed since the demolition action was completed, it was conceivable that the torpedo boats had already begun to move and this sort of stir was quite capable of setting off the mines. In the meantime, a glimmer of light was observed from the roof of the operation room at Ras Sudr. However, it did not arouse any suspicions concerning the cause of the explosion because these sorts of flashes and bursts of light were rather commonplace in the region.

At 0310, pig #4 linked up with the IDF Bertram boat that had set out to meet it. Two minutes later, the demolition officer, Israel Roth, who was positioned on the roof, reported that he noticed a gleam of light flare up about twenty miles away, from the direction of the torpedo boats' place of anchorage. We surmised that the flash derived from the detonation of the planted mines, and military intelligence later confirmed our assumption. Fifteen minutes later, at 0330, pig #4 reached Ras Sudr.

Given the thirty-minute time difference between the demolition actions of each crew, there still wasn't any reason to worry about pig #3. However, the second explosion raised doubts, and we sent out search teams fifteen minutes after the first pig returned. Bertram boats and rubber crafts began to comb the pigs' designated route, and a helicopter—carrying Dr. Slavin, Gadi Kroll, and myself—hedge-hopped over the coastline and to the north. In addition, a light patrol plane scanned the strip of sea parallel to the coastline and its immediate environs. No one noticed the distress flares that were activated by the staff of pig #3, and there were no calls for help over the wireless. As it turned out, the communication device was destroyed in the explosion on board the missing pig.

At 0830, the four commandos from pig #3 were found floating in the water. Only Aryo, among the Shayetet's most strapping *lochamim*, was still alive. Aryo caught the pilot's attention by generating foam on the surface of the sea with his hands, directing the helicopter to the location. Upon reaching the scene, the helicopter crew lowered Gadi Kroll down to the water on a cable, and he reported that only Aryo had survived. Gadi then immediately lifted the veteran pigist to the helicopter with the help of the cable.

Aryo treaded water for no fewer than six hours and fifteen minutes, despite having his jaw broken in the blast. Throughout that time, he looked after his comrades, two of whom died in his hands. Notwithstanding his perilous state, Aryo insisted that we lift his fallen comrades to the chopper before evacuating him to the hospital, as he was worried that sharks would feast on his fellow crew members. By the time Aryo was pulled out of the sea, he was enervated and on the verge of losing consciousness. When I realized

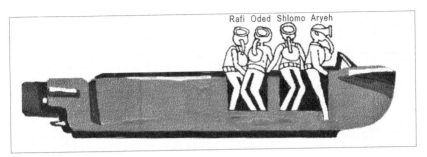

Seating order on board "pig" before explosion.

Operation Escort—The operators of "pig" #4 meet with the Admiral of the Navy and the Shayetet's commander at Ras Sudr after the mission.

that his friends were no longer among the living, my top priority was to make sure that Aryo survived. Therefore, I wanted to evacuate him to the hospital at once. I consulted with Dr. Shimon Slavin, who was in the process of examining him, and the doctor decided that we could wait with the evacuation until the three bodies were salvaged from the sea.

If not for Aryo's insatiable will to survive and unworldly dedication to his comrades, it is almost certain that we would never have figured out what had become of the ill-fated crew of pig #3 on its way back from Operation Escort 2, or the source of the explosion. What's more, the report that Aryo submitted prevented additional tragedies in the future.

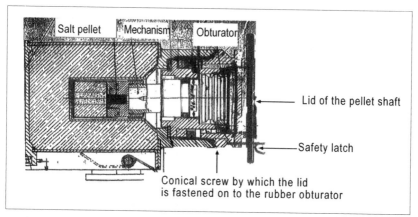

Mechanism of the limpet mine

Aryo personally informed us that the pig's self-destruct mine,[8] which was strapped to its designated spot above the engine tanks and behind the passengers' compartment, went off on its own. Rafi Miloh, who was closest to the mine, was killed on the spot, while Oded Nir and Shlomo Eshel, who were sitting before Rafi in single file, were badly wounded and eventually lost too much blood. In essence, the three passengers dampened the force of the blast with their bodies. By the time it got to Aryo, in the front compartment by the wheel, the blast had lost some of its bite and this is what saved his life.

The tragic incident was investigated by both the Shayetet's engineers and a specially appointed Navy commission. According to the findings, the engineering structure of the mine's pellet shaft was faulty. The conical aluminum cover was sealed with a lid that was screwed onto the grooves along the top edges of the shaft and was fastened onto a rubber O-ring that encased the base of the cone. Due to pig #3's prolonged stay of over ten hours in the sea, the inadequate insulation failed to prevent water from penetrating the shaft. The water subsequently caused the salt pellet in the mine's activation mechanism to melt, thereby triggering the lethal blast. The findings made it clear that the insulation of the pellet shaft was predicated on the amount of pressure that was brought to bear when the section was initially sealed and fastened. Needless to say, the pressure was not enough to withstand the rigors of the voyage.

The design of the faulty mine was based on the lessons that were gleaned from a similar incident during Operation Kadesh (the Israeli part of the 1956

Sinai Crisis), in which no lives were lost. However, it turned out that the engineers who planned the mine in the early 1960s failed to thoroughly implement that same lesson, as their design ultimately failed to prevent water from infiltrating the shaft.

The tragedy was all the more serious, for the self-destruct mine was a standard feature that was installed into every pig. As such, it had passed all the formal quality-control tests that were conducted by the authorized bodies, such as Navy Headquarters, RAFAEL (the Armament Development Authority), and the Ordinance Corps. What's more, it was designed by the Shayetet's gifted chief engineer, who had studied mechanical engineering and served as a demolition officer. Ironically, he received the Israel Defense Award for the development of this very mine. Notwithstanding all the accolades, this mine killed three outstanding *lochamim*, who were destined for bright futures in the S-13. To add insult to injury, their young lives came to an awful end a mere two hours after they had completed the most challenging operational part of the mission: planting the mines on the targets.

We immediately began to plan and produce a new mine, so that we would never again have to bear a "ticking bomb" on our backs. The new mine possessed a cylindrical pellet shaft, which was sealed on top of an O-ring that enveloped the entire cover. Consequently, the O-ring secured the mine's insulation on its own, without having to depend on the strength with which the lid was fastened over the cylinder and ring.

Results of the Mission

Operation Escort 2 came to a close with the planting and activation of all eight limpet mines on the two Egyptian torpedo boats. The divers also managed to activate five of the attendant anti-removal systems. As a result, the two enemy ships were detonated and sunk. With the torpedo boats out of the way, the armored landing and assault—within the framework of Operation Raviv—was launched and managed to take the enemy completely by surprise.

From an operational standpoint, Operation Escort was considered a huge success. The mission was accomplished despite the extraordinary difficulties and circumstances that we were forced to work under. However, the tragic death of three of our comrades-in-arms cast a dark veil over the formidable achievement. We were left with a bitter sense of impotence and glaring injustice, for these men executed the mission in a nigh-flawless manner, only to have their lives cut short by a technical malfunction, which stemmed from developments that long predated the mission itself and had nothing to do with our preparations. Both the admiral of the Navy and the IDF commander in chief expressed similar sentiments in their letters of commendation.

Avraham Botzer's Letter:

Commander of the S-13
Subject: Operation Escort

With the successful conclusion of the operations, the sinking of the torpedo boats and the assault on the beaches of Egypt, I would like to express to you, and through you to all those who took part in Operation Escort, my esteem for the planning, preparations, and perfect execution of the operation.

The mission constituted a condition without which it would have been impossible to carry out the assault. The sinking of the torpedo boats was executed under difficult condition—a dearth of information, long distances, the enemy's heightened state of alert, and heavy currents.

The mission was fulfilled thanks to the dedication of all those who participated in it, primarily the perseverance and steadfastness of the men in the field. This was the first time in the annals of the IDF and the Navy in which enemy war vessels were sunk by means of a frogman operation.

The Navy and I share in the unit's pain over the accident and the loss of three of the unit's *lochamim* who took part in the mission. May we no longer know such tragedy.

A. Botzer, Rear Admiral
Admiral of the Navy

Haim Bar-Lev's Letter:

Sept. 12, 1969
Commander of the Shayetet 13
[c.c.:] Commander of the Navy
Subject: Operation Escort

The mission to sink the Egyptian torpedo boats in the Gulf of Suez was the first of its kind to be carried out by the Shayetet. The sinking of the torpedo boats was a *condition* for the execution of Raviv, which was similarly a unique and unprecedented operation. The Shayetet was equal to the task, which this time around entailed an exceptionally difficult professional test.

Both professionals and layman alike sense the physical, mental, and technical difficulties that the operation demanded and appreciate the fitness, perseverance, valor of spirit, dedication, and wisdom of those that brought it to fruition.

With all the sorrow and anguish over the death of LCdr Rafi Miloh, First Lt Shlomo Eshel, and CPO Oded Nir, who fell as a result of a technical malfunction after fulfilling the mission, I would like to express my esteem to you and through you to the Shayetet—first and foremost to those men that personally carried out the mission—for this accomplishment.

Haim Bar-Lev, Lieutenant General
Chief of the General Staff

Operation Escort was a living embodiment of the "special military operation," namely an action conducted behind enemy lines with a relatively small force and limited means, in pursuit of an objective possessing far-ranging military and/or political significance. The central feature of a special operation is the element of surprise. In Operation Escort, the Navy Commando took advantage of the maritime theater in order to catch the enemy off guard within its own territorial waters.

The sinking of the Egyptian torpedo boats was preceded by the Shayetet's raids against land-based targets in which the assailing force pounced on the enemy from the sea. These ground operations essentially set the stage for the General Staff's decision to entrust the Shayetet with a classic and targeted naval commando operation—Operation Escort. The S-13 thereby proved the righteousness of the path that it had embarked on sixteen months earlier when we decided to plunge into the field of infantry combat. By dint of this undertaking, the Shayetet merited recognition as an elite operational unit, whose skills and input are in high demand.

Operation Escort set new standards of excellence. The Shayetet developed and availed itself of novel and daring techniques and methods of operation. Moreover, during the raid, the commandos exemplified the combat norms and values, such as unstinting adherence to the mission, professionalism, discipline, and sacrifice, which were prerequisites for overcoming the obstacles and attaining the mission's objective.

Over the course of the War of Attrition, the S-13 set new standards, developed an array of methods and means, and carried out myriad actions. These resources constituted a "combat arsenal" and infrastructure that endowed the unit with the flexibility to operate in every facet of war. Furthermore, the S-13's performance in the War of Attrition placed the entire Navy on "the IDF's operational map," as Operation Escort and Operation Raviv marked the first time the Corps was integrated as an important and prerequisite factor in a large and successful offensive. As a result of these achievements, the General Staff granted the Navy the freedom of action to operate maritime vessels and conduct special missions in the Yom Kippur War and beyond.

Rear Admiral (Res.) Ami Ayalon's Outlook on Operation Escort

Rear Admiral (Res.) Ami Ayalon was the commander of one of the two pig crews that sank the pair of Egyptian torpedo boats near Ras Sadat, in the northern Gulf of Suez. Ami Ayalon also took part in the raids on the Ras Adabiyah Coastal Station and the Green Island Fortress, where he served as a young officer and was badly wounded. For his role in Green Island, Ayalon was decorated with the Medal of Valor. In days to come, he was to be appointed the commander of the Shayetet 13 and the admiral of the Navy.

Following is Ami Ayalon's contribution to the aforementioned seminar "Special Operations in the War of Israel from 1943 to 1981":

> I do not intend on telling the story of the operation or the battle. Rear Admiral Ze'ev Almog, who was my commander before, during, and after (in the Red Sea Arena) the mission, has already provided us with an in-depth view. For the sake of elucidating the fact that there is more than one vantage point, I would like to complement Ze'ev's account with a couple of personal insights. This is not to say that there is a "Rashomon" here; I merely wish to present certain aspects from the perspective of

someone who observed the mission from beneath the water, instead of from the standpoint of the planning and execution.

Looking back from a distance of several decades at the tens or hundreds of missions that I participated in during my lifetime, Operation Escort was one of the most innovative, if not the most innovative mission of them all. Although it was ostensibly a classic naval commando operation, in my opinion it does not match the criteria of a classic operation, for it involved a great deal of daring, even though none of the participants received a citation. In fact, it was one of the more audacious missions that I have ever participated in from the standpoint of the personal ability and courage that was required of all the people who took part in it—from all of the eight lochamim that were on the front line of combat.

At the time, we—and I am primarily referring to us eight lochamim—were accompanied by two feelings: the first was that everything was riding on our shoulders. This sense of duty was an extremely powerful presence throughout the War of Attrition, and we held many conversations about this topic among ourselves. The second feeling, which was crucial and is worth going into, was that "our failure during the Six Day War would never happen again." More specifically, we would not return to the days when the members of the S-13 had to explain to debriefers why we did not carry out the mission, to include those that I participated in myself. This sense of failure is one of the two central factors that paved the way for the planning, ingenuity, daring, and perseverance that were detailed in such a lucid fashion by Rear Admiral Ze'ev Almog.

It is also worth noting that we never trained for a mission along the lines of Escort, even in general exercises. Our conduct in the operation itself was dictated to us from the command post—from Ze'ev Almog—by an order that we received to enter minimal buoyancy mode. Minimal buoyancy against a northerly wind obligates you to submerge, in other words, to assume a position where your head is rarely above the water. In practice, only "Fatty" (Eldad Dinur), the pig's commander, had his head above the surface. Fatty, who even then was a rather broad guy, took up quite a bit of the vehicle's limited space. Originally, the pig was intended for only two commandos and we squeezed in four. The significance of entering minimal buoyancy was that we were basically attached to the breathing set throughout the twelve hours that we were in the vehicle. We did, however, occasionally go up for some fresh air because there wasn't enough oxygen in the tank.

There is one key innovation that was developed by the S-13 during the run-up to the mission that Ze'ev Almog did not expand on, and you may have picked up on it between the lines: I'm talking about using pigs in deep-water attacks. The pig is a vehicle that ordinarily lands on the seabed. However, human beings need clean oxygen, and breathing oxygen at an atmospheric pressure of over 0.7—a depth of twenty-three feet—is liable to expose divers to the grave dangers of oxygen toxicity, whose symptoms include epileptic attacks and loss of consciousness. (I don't suggest that any of you try this at home.) Therefore, an effort is usually made to dive at depths that are shallower than twenty-three to twenty-six feet. Since it was clear that the attack on the Egyptian torpedo boats would involve landing the pig at greater depths (and this is indeed what happened in practice), we developed a method that enabled the pig to reach what is called "minimal flotation" with "half flash" (a technical detail that pertains to the mode of operation). Shlomo Asif ("Bigler"), who was our pig's driver, was charged with carrying this out and his professional ability enabled us to pull it off. In a mission like Escort, you basically create positive flotation by balancing the vehicle with the head of the pig's commander. The moment his head sticks out of the water, the specific weight (gravity) is altered and the vehicle basically rotates between a state of positive and negative flotation. This is a very delicate state that is dependent on the driver's instincts, and not the vehicle's dials.

The S-13 came up with numerous revolutionary methods and tools for the mission. These innovations demanded a very high professional level, yet only a few of the unit's men were at such a level during that same period.

When you talk about the S-13, what comes to my mind is the group of twenty-four commandos who were on the front line of Adabiyah and Green Island. Four of these same men were in the vanguard of Operation Escort, and they were the ones who executed most of the actions during the mission. We are not dealing with tens or hundreds of soldiers here.

It must also be remembered that out of the twenty combatants who were in the first wave of fighting at Green Island, about ten were injured and only four made it off the island unscathed. As Ze'ev Almog mentioned, I personally ended up in the hospital and was then sent to recuperate in Kay House.[9]

If truth be told, at the time I was not driven by the stuff that they write about in books; we did what we did out of a vague sense that everything—the security of the State of Israel—was resting on our shoulders. This may sound exceedingly "high-minded," but I believe that this is what motivated this young group. The primary reason for this sense of responsibility was that after the Six Day War practically all of Israel's borders abutted bodies of water, including the Jordan River. Therefore, the Shayetet's young and small band of commandos took part in nearly all of the IDF's missions during that same period (with the exception of helicopter operations). We basically did it out of a sense of duty and lack of choice.

The heavy workload on the pig unit severely wore down its soldiers, not to mention the men who were injured on Green Island. To a certain extent, the workload and fatigue were also responsible for the fact that, for all intents and purposes, the unit lacked a commander. Therefore, Ze'ev Almog, in his capacity as the head of the Shayetet, did the right and nearly only possible thing when he brought Shlomo Eshel back from home to lead the pigists. I was unaware of the talks that Ze'ev held with Shlomo in order to convince him to return. In the end, the *mighty* pig unit had between two and four individuals whose professional level was on par with the needs of the mission.

It is important to emphasize that Shlomo Eshel was indeed an extraordinary man of exceptional courage, but his professional skills were extremely rusty, simply because he had been out of action. Diving is the sort of activity where if you don't practice four nights a week, you're not going to be ready for this sort of a mission. Shlomo's less than adequate state of fitness came into play on the first night of the operation, when the Egyptian torpedo boats, which were *not* anchored in their place, opened fire and charged at us. In the final equation, the initial reaction of the second pig to the enemy's approach was highly unprofessional and Ze'ev Almog considered replacing the crew.

Of all the pig commanders during that same period, in my estimation only Fatty and Aryeh Yitzchak were at the necessary level of execution. Both of them were seasoned senior chief petty officers who constituted the true backbone of the Shayetet in all that concerned professional ability. The officers, myself included, were men with a great deal of originality, creativity, and courage, but our professional level, especially when it came to operating the vehicles, did not reach the ankles of these senior NCOs (non-commissioned officers), who basically carried the unit on their shoulders. I would like to add that Aryeh, who is quite a character in his own right, largely made up for and complimented Shlomo Eshel's professional shortcomings; it was Aryeh who ultimately enabled that vehicle to reach an extremely high level of execution, which was demonstarated during the mission itself.

There was also a problem putting together the force. Ze'ev Almog emphasized the fact that I showed up at his office and he sent me—rightly so—to the doctor, who, after a bit of persuasion, said that everything was all right. It must be remembered that there were very few people—to put it lightly—who wanted to participate in this operation, as the Shayetet's small group of commandos was worn out by the heavy operational workload. Although I had to fight with Ze'ev to let me join the force, I didn't have to compete for my spot with the soldiers in the unit, even though I had run away from Kay House. I'm not bringing this up in order to sing my own praises, but to emphasize just how great the workload was on an extremely small group of men.

Operation Escort was beset by a host of technical problems. Three soldiers were killed as a result of an error in the engineering design of a mine, which only came to our attention after the fact. There were also difficulties planting mines on maritime vessels made of wood, and Ze'ev Almog has discussed these issues at length. In the end, only a fraction of the mines at our disposal met our operational standards for planting the limpets.

The personal experience of landing underwater after hours of not being able to see a thing, due to the fact that we were in a submerged state (the only one who could see was the vehicle commander), was quite unique. At the outset, the plan was for the pig to enter "minimal flotation," but we ended up landing the vehicle. When Fatty told Avishai and me to head in a particular direction, we exited the vehicle and rose to the surface for one last peek. At the surface, our eyes honed in on what is the dream of every frogman: the targets—the silhouette of those same ships that we had searched for the previous night and which fired in our direction and went berserk above us, while activating their propellers. This situation is not easy to describe. Everything that followed seemed almost simple in comparison, including most of the technical problems that we encountered while planting the mines and the complications with the tape line.

Avishai and I returned, waving the mine's safety pins—a frogman's most treasured possession—to the vehicle, which waited for us at a depth of around thirty-three feet. However, when we got to the pig, we faced the most dangerous obstacle of them all: Fatty's hug. It is difficult to fathom what it's like to be hugged by Fatty at such depths. The man practically ripped the breathing set off of my mouth. In any event, we overcame that scare as well.

The tragedy that struck the second pig has already been discussed. At the time of the explosion, the crew members of the first pig, myself included, were still out at sea. When we heard the blast, we assumed that the torpedo boats had been sunk and screamed for joy. Only later did we understand that it was, in fact, the second pig that had gone up in smoke. The moment we realized what had actually happened was one of the saddest in my entire life.

Besides the two feelings that accompanied us as combat soldiers—the unit's dismal performance in the Six Day War and our guarantee that it would never happen again; and the sense that everything was riding on our shoulders—we also drew important conclusions from Operation Escort in all that concerned combat doctrine, planning (to include dynamic adjustments over the course of the mission), and how the intelligence picture falls into place during the weeks before an operation. These lessons had a tremendous impact on me. In the days to come, I drew on these same lessons as the commander of the S-13 and the admiral of the Navy.

The way I see it, the battle against the torpedo boats was decided at least a year earlier when Ze'ev Almog built the new cadre of officers that went on to lead the Shayetet in the War of Attrition and the subsequent campaigns. His decision was a very important phase in my personal development and, in my estimation, that of the entire S-13. This group of officers was chosen and educated against the backdrop of a real and painful effort to draw conclusions. My formative experience as an officer took place during a staff commanders course (or what we referred to then as a company commanders course) that Ze'ev Almog presided over. He took the Shayetet's operations in the Six Day War—missions in which the unit did not achieve its objectives from both the standpoint of the commandos' personal ability, the planning on the part of the command echelons, and every other aspect as well—and analyzed them in the most excruciating way possible. For all intents and purposes, we (myself included) had repressed the Shayetet's failure from the Six Day War until the moment we convened for that same staff commanders course in 1969. The capacity to analyze the failures of every operation and think about how they should have been planned, prepared, and conducted (including the decisions that were made over the course of the mission) was no less than my formative experience as an officer. I know that these lessons influenced many of my actions in Operation Escort and later missions too. In my opinion, this course was not only the formative experience of my career, but the same can be said for the entire Shayetet 13.

FOUR

The S-13's Operations at the Hurgada Anchorage during the Yom Kippur War

The Hurgada Anchorage was the focal point of the Navy Commando's operations during the Yom Kippur War. Despite the inferiority of our forces, the four raids that were conducted against Hurgada bolstered our operational and strategic status quo vis à vis the Egyptians on the Red Sea front immensely. These missions were a natural continuation of the Shayetet's operations during the War of Attrition, some four years earlier. At Hurgada, we reaped the harvest of the experience and self-confidence that was acquired in the War of Attrition.

Over the course of the Yom Kippur War, I served as the naval commander of the Red Sea Theater (the IDF zone of command that encompassed the Sinai Peninsula). In that capacity, I presided over the majority of the S-13's combat force, including many of the outstanding officers and combat soldiers who fought under my command in the War of Attrition. I felt privileged to receive another opportunity to put the virtues of these wonderful soldiers to good use during the darkest and most fateful hours of the Yom Kippur War.

The Hurgada Anchorage overlooks the maritime junction where the northern Red Sea and southern tip of the Gulf of Suez converge. The control over this crossroads constitutes one of the keys to ascendancy over the entire area. The Shayetet's four raids against Hurgada epitomize the utility and value that can be generated from these sorts of "special operations." In fact, during that same period, the IDF lacked any other alternative for attacking this critical installation.

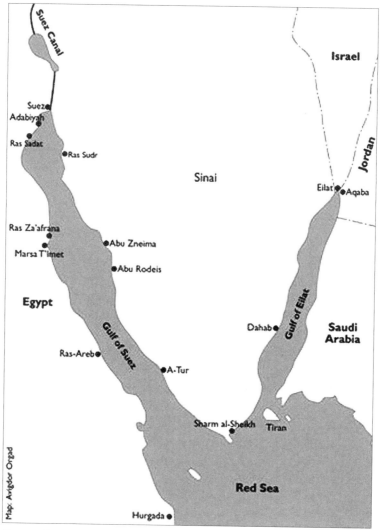

Theater of combat.

Across the sea from Hurgada lies Sharm al-Sheikh, which was then under Israeli control. Sharm al-Sheikh is perched over the confluence of three major seaways: to its north is a route that leads to the Mediterranean Sea and the Atlantic Ocean, via the Gulf of Suez and its eponymous canal; to the south, the Red Sea links up with the Indian Ocean; and to the northeast, the Gulf of Eilat serves as Saudi Arabia's northern outlet and Jordan and Israel's lone outlet to the south. Sharm al-Sheikh's geographical location, at the northern tip of the Red Sea, thus conferred on it a unique international importance as well as an advantage over the Hurgada Anchorage: control over the entrance to the Gulf of Eilat.

From a military-strategic perspective, Israel's control over this maritime junction as well as *Merchav Shlomo* (the "Solomon Region," the Israeli name for the southern Sinai), and the Sharm al-Sheikh Anchorage provided us with a clear-cut strategic edge over the Egyptians, due to the following reasons:

- The master of this junction controlled the north-bound sea routes and the northern entrance to the Red Sea. This enabled the IDF to prevent ships from passing through this crossroads.
- It constituted a relatively facile stepping-stone into the heart of Egypt, from which we could cut off the Arab Republic's upper half from its lower. Moreover, it enabled the IDF to array its forces opposite Cairo.
- This crossroads allowed the IDF to execute a strategic flanking movement against the rear of the Egyptian Army, which was deployed along the length of the Suez Canal, via the empty expanses of desert that run parallel to and west of the Gulf of Suez.

Israel's control over this strategic point thus posed a palpable strategic threat to Egypt's security. Our presence in the Sinai Peninsula constituted a significant stumbling block to the Republic's quest for power and status, for it was dependent on a foreign factor, namely Israel, with which it could purportedly never have relations. Even so, Sharm al-Sheikh and *Merchav Shlomo* were cut off from Israel by a vast desert. Its strategic importance, distance from supply sources, and lack of convenient means of transportation whetted Egypt's appetite to reclaim its former territory. Consequently, our deployment in the Red Sea Theater was geared toward the following objectives: defending Israel's strategic assets (the straits and oil deposits) in the Gulf of Suez, the Gulf of Eilat, and Sharm al-Sheikh; protecting *Merchav Shlomo* against attacks from the sea; and upholding the principle of freedom of shipping. It was also obvious that we had to prepare for inevitable war.

Assignments in the Red Sea Theater before the War

Before the Yom Kippur War, the Red Sea Theater Headquarters was charged with two central missions:

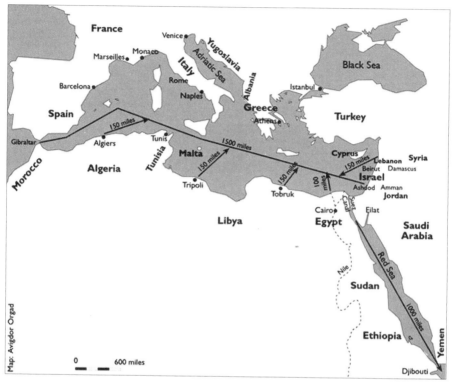

Maritime theater.

- To establish infrastructure for the absorption of six new missile boats (*Saa'r* 4's) into the theater's disposition of forces.
- To prepare for Operation Ohr Yarok (green light)—the landing of an armored division, in shifts, on the southwestern coast of the Gulf of Suez.[1]

The six missile boats were slated to leave Haifa, circle Africa, and reach Sharm al-Sheikh. However, the Yom Kippur War broke out a mere nine days before the first two boats were scheduled to set sail, and they would only reach the area a half year after the war. As a result, Theater Headquarters had to reconcile itself with the fact that it would not have any missile boats throughout the course of the war.

As noted above, Operation Ohr Yarok was deemed to be a principal task of the Red Sea Theater before the war, so that the designated mission was well planned and drilled. In fact the operation was even showcased before

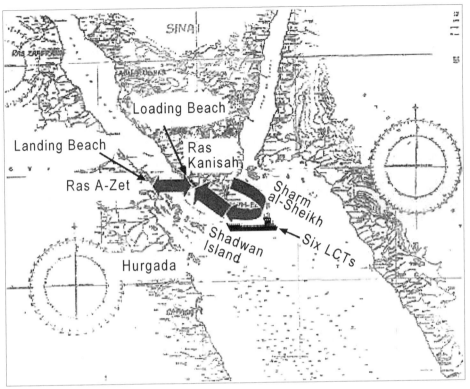

Operation Ohr Yarok—Landing of an armored division.

the General Staff within the framework of a general exercise ("Medakdek," stickler) on August 2, 1973. During the war, the SOP for Ohr Yarok was commenced and then suspended on three separate occasions, before ultimately being scrapped.

As such, the two principal missions that the Red Sea Theater was primed for—landing the armored division and operating missile boats in the arena—did not come to fruition during the war. Nevertheless, the theater's primary objectives—defending the shipping lanes, preserving the IDF's freedom of action in the Gulf of Suez, and safeguarding Israel's strategic assets in the region—were fully accomplished. These achievements could be largely credited to small naval forces that were placed at the Red Sea Theater's disposal during the war, as these units carried out multiple offensive actions against Egyptian targets, foremost among them the S-13's raids against the Hurgada Anchorage.

The Balance of Power in the Region

From early 1973 until the eve of the war, the IDF's forces in *Merchav Shlomo* and the Red Sea Theater were decidedly outclassed by those of the enemy. Israel had the following military resources in the region:

- On Land: About thirty Sherman tanks and one to two reserve infantry regiments.
- In the Air: For most of the war, the Red Sea Theater had to make do with a pair of Phantom jets, alongside a Hawk ground-to-air missile battery at Sharm al-Sheikh and another at Ras Sudr.
- At Sea: Although the maritime front was 375 miles long and included the entire Gulf of Suez (a relatively narrow sea route that was nearly 220 nautical miles long and surrounded by desert on either side), our entire fleet consisted of five *Dabour* boats, only four of which were manned; four *Tsir'ah* light patrol boats, which were transferred from Ras Sudr to Eilat in May 1973; a *Bat-Sheva* 325-foot LCT (landing craft—tanks and troop carriers), three 120-foot LCTs, and two *Shikma* 239-foot LCTs, for a grand total of six aging crafts (which were capable of landing thirty-seven *Tiran* tanks[2] and thirty-one armored personnel carriers in one wave); and one auxiliary ship, the INS *Bat-Yam*. If truth be told, the *Bat-Yam* was more of a burden than an asset. Due to its hefty bulk and light weaponry, we were forced to take measures to "hide" the ship throughout the war, lest it fall in harm's way.

On the eve of the war, the Red Sea Theater's forces were basically suited for defensive patrols and transport duties in the vicinity of the Sinai beaches—not offensive assignments. However, even our means for defending *Merchav Shlomo* left much to be desired. The number of ground and naval tools that stood at our disposal was rather meager and lagged behind the enemy's from a technological standpoint, and our airborne force was miniscule. These limited resources were pitted against a large Egyptian Navy, which was primarily geared for the offensive.

In contrast, during the war, Egypt could avail itself of the following forces in the Gulf of Suez:

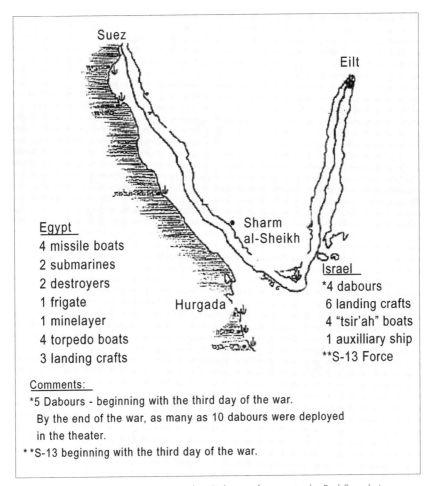

Suez

Eilt

Sharm
al-Sheikh

Hurgada

Egypt
4 missile boats
2 submarines
2 destroyers
1 frigate
1 minelayer
4 torpedo boats
3 landing crafts

Israel
*4 dabours
6 landing crafts
4 "tsir'ah" boats
1 auxilliary ship
**S-13 Force

Comments:
*5 Dabours - beginning with the third day of the war.
 By the end of the war, as many as 10 dabours were deployed
 in the theater.
**S-13 beginning with the third day of the war.

The Shayetet 13's operations at Hurgada—Balance of power in the Red Sea during the Yom Kippur War.

- In their anchorages (Adabiyah, Marsa T'lmet, and Ras-Areb), the Egyptians had access to a fleet of about one hundred fishing boats, which could be readily conscripted for logistical purposes, such as transferring combat equipment, supplies, and troops to Sinai's beaches.
- Commando units in Adabiyah and Marsa T'lmet, which moved about in five Bertram boats and rubber crafts.
- Two K-123 torpedo boats and two De Castro patrol boats at Adabiyah.
- A coastal array of radar-controlled 130-mm shore guns at Ras Machgara and 25-pound guns at Ras Zafarana.

The *Dabour* patrol boat.

- Armored infantry regiments that patrolled along the coast and rear of the anchorages at Marsa T'lmet and Ras-Areb.
- Above all, Egypt's missile boats constituted a qualitative advantage that shifted the balance of power decisively in its favor, especially since the IDF did not have any missile boats in the theater.

The Egyptians leaned on three important naval bases in the area of the Red Sea south of the Gulf of Suez:[3]

- Hurgada was Egypt's frontline military anchorage in the northern Red Sea, as it overlooked the entrance to the Gulf and constituted a threat to Sharm al-Sheikh. Moreover, it was a fortified and heavily-guarded installation.
- Safaga—30 miles south of Hurgada.
- Ras Banas—250 miles south of Sharm al-Sheikh.

The Egyptian naval forces in the Red Sea were primarily charged with imposing a naval blockade on Israel and helping the ground forces capture the south of Sinai and *Merchav Shlomo*.[4]

THE EGYPTIAN MISSILE THREAT

Given the lack of IDF missile boats at the Red Sea front, the principal threat that we faced was the enemy's own missiles. In essence, the Egyptians established a pair of missile-defended zones between Hurgada and the Sinai coast. An aerial missile-defended zone with a radius of twenty-two nautical miles (roughly twenty-five standard miles) was enforced from Hurgada to Shadwan Island. The zone was comprised of a network of six SA-2 and SA-3 ground-to-air missile batteries, which were arrayed in an arch-like formation around Hurgada. The second field was a maritime missile-defended zone that extended from Shadwan Island to the Sinai coast. The maritime zone was predicated on Styx missiles, which were mounted on the decks of the enemy's missile boats and had a range of twenty-five nautical miles.

Egypt's aerial and maritime missile-defended zones were intended to seal off the IDF's aerial and maritime outlets. In the absence of Israeli missile boats, Egyptian missiles indeed threatened every Israeli plane or boat that passed

Egyptian naval forces arrayed in the Red Sea during the Yom Kippur War.

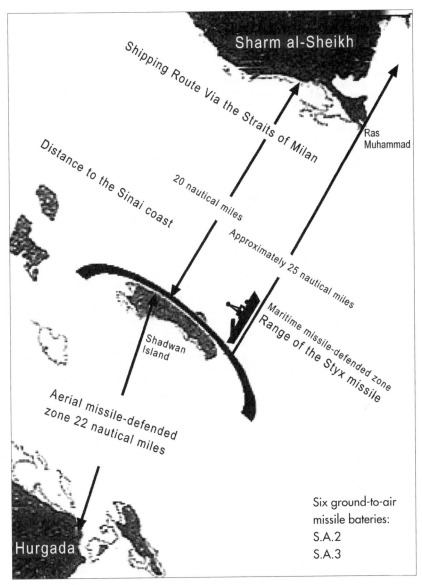

The Egyptian missile boats and ground-to-air missile threat.

through this area. If Israel failed to remove the missile threat, Israeli Air Force (IAF) jets and Israeli surface vehicles would not be able to attack Hurgada or the Egyptian missile boats, which were launching missiles at IDF forces passing through the Gulf. What's more, the IAF claimed that it would need tens of fighter jets to eliminate the enemy's ground-to-air missile batteries.

Another consequence of these integrated air and maritime antimissile defense zones was that Egyptian missile boats, equipped with Styx missiles, could navigate their way from Hurgada to Shadwan Island with relative ease without being detected or threatened. By hugging the island's shoreline, Egyptian missile boats could ambush Israeli maritime vessels that tried to pass through the Gulf of Suez. One Styx missile carrying 500 kg of heavy explosives was capable of sinking a landing craft, such as the INS *Bat-Sheva*, along with the 41 armored vehicles and 400 soldiers that the ship carried.

On the very first day of the war, the IAF launched an unsuccessful attack on the Egyptian missile boats cruising on the open seas. In consequence, the enemy vessels managed to attack five IDF boats that were on patrol along the coast of Sharm al-Sheikh. Had the boats not taken evasive action, they would certainly have been destroyed.

So long as the Egyptians maintained their missile capabilities, Israeli naval vessels would be precluded from entering or exiting the Gulf of Suez and our freedom of action would have been limited to a narrow strip nearly 220 miles long. As it was, the Red Sea Theater—*Merchav Shlomo* in general and Sharm al-Sheikh in particular—had vastly limited means for protecting the region. This state of affairs not only jeopardized the planned landing of an armored division in the southwestern Gulf of Suez, but raised serious doubts concerning the IDF's ability to fend off the Egyptians' attempt to conquer the area.

THE RESPONSE: CATCHING THE ENEMY OFF GUARD WITH SPECIAL OPERATIONS

The predicament that we found ourselves in essentially dictated the need for a special operation: the tactical use of "a small force and limited means," while focusing on mental and psychological principles that would enable us to anticipate the enemy's pattern of behavior and reactions. The impact of a special operation was likely to transcend the mission's quantitative results and thus provide an effective response to the Egyptian offensive.

My underlying premise was that the greater the defenses at a target, the more its guards tend to place their trust on the network of fortifications. These very advantages tend to blur the defenders' sight, so that they have a hard time discerning the cracks in their armor. On the other hand, the raider must locate these cracks and display the wherewithal to exploit them. A successful surprise attack dazes the target's complacent defenders, blunting the troops' instincts, and slowing down their reaction time. Consequently, a small and inferior force can get away after delivering the blow.

In my estimation, the Hurgada Anchorage was the epitome of a highly fortified and remote target that is practically begging to be infiltrated and hammered time and again by a slippery, sophisticated, and miniscule force. In retrospect, this course of action ultimately caused the hitherto complacent defenders at Hurgada to pick up and leave the strategically invaluable position.

Historical Background of the Hurgada Raids

In 1956, at the height of Operation Kadesh, Izy Rahav, the commander of the S-13, stood by the hatch of a C-47 Skytrain cargo plane with four Shayetet commandos. The force was slated to parachute into the sea, alongside their kayaks, and carry out an attack on Sharm al-Sheikh, which was in Egypt's hands until 1967. However, the mission was aborted because the pilots were uncertain as to whether they had positively identified the drop point.

In 1960, during my tenure as the commander of the Shayetet's divers unit, we carried out numerous "model drills" for a strike against Hurgada, so that I was well versed with the target. Within the framework of these exercises, the force would depart from Ramat David[5] on board a C-47 and parachute into the sea, along with kayaks. The troops would then paddle within "foot" range of the target, before swimming and diving the rest of the way. After planting limpet mines onto boats, the divers would be picked up on the outskirts of the target by choppers. Although the operation demanded a grueling physical effort of the commandos, it was within the realm of the possible. The senior brass considered executing this sort of a mission in the Six Day War, and one was ultimately conducted in Alexandria by the S-13's Divers Company.

On February 6, 1970, in the midst of the War of Attrition, the IAF attacked the Hurgada Anchorage and sunk a minelayer, in retaliation for the damage exacted by Egyptian frogmen on the naval boats INS *Bat-Galim* and *Bat-Sheva* in Eilat.[6] Egyptian missile boats struck back on May 13, 1970, by sinking the *Orit*, an Israeli fishing boat, in the southeastern Mediterranean, off Lake Bardawil in the northern Sinai. Two days later, Egyptian frogmen planted limpet mines on the aforementioned *Bat-Galim*, which was capsized

An S-13 operation ("model") at Hurgada—Kayaks parachuted into the sea.

on the seabed of the Navy's anchorage in Eilat. The mines went off, leaving one civilian dead and two wounded. Incidentally, the three casualties were reserve soldiers in the S-13, who were salvaging the ship for a commercial contractor.

Lieutenant Ilan Egozi, in his capacity as the commander of the Divers Company, and the author, while still serving as the S-13's commander, planned to retaliate for the two attacks on Eilat by launching a raid against Egyptian naval boats in the Ras Banas Anchorage. The mission was assigned to the Shayetet because, at the time, Ras Banas was on the outer limits of the IAF combat jets' range. Over the course of the SOP, we parachuted forces and their attendant rubber crafts from a Nord plane three times (in the presence of Raful, who was still serving as the Chief Infantry and Paratroopers Officer). Despite the fact that the method was long considered to be standard practice, the boats kept shattering into pieces upon hitting the water (the engineering design of the parachuting system turned out to be faulty). Consequently, it was the IAF that launched Operation Keshet Avirit (airborne arch), the strike against the Egyptian anchorage at Ras Banas on May 16. Israeli combat jets sank a Z-class destroyer and a Komar missile boat, damaged a landing craft, and exacted about thirty Egyptian casualties. In the aftermath of Keshet Avirit, the Egyptians fortified the Hurgada Anchorage with six SA-2 and SA-3 batteries and a squadron of MIGs.

By 1972, the situation at Hurgada and its environs had dramatically changed. Although the S-13's starting line was now Sharm al-Sheikh, instead of distant Atlit, overall the conditions for launching an attack on Hurgada were more difficult. Egypt's aerial missile-defended zone ruled out all assistance—be it transportation, offensive actions, and rescue missions—within its boundaries. Likewise, the maritime missile-defended zone precluded the Red Sea Theater's naval surface vehicles (*Dabour* boats and the *Bat-Yam* auxiliary ship) from offering transportation support and carrying out offensive or rescue operations.

Nevertheless, the S-13 could draw on several advantages that did not exist in the past. The Shayetet had already acquired *Snuniyot* and Mark V rubber crafts, which were capable of crossing the sea, reaching distant Hurgada, and then entering the anchorage surreptitiously. During the War of Attrition, the S-13 amassed a treasure trove of first-rate operational experience, both on land and at sea. Additionally, the Shayetet's *lochamim* had proven their operational mettle, especially in the raids against Adabiyah and Green Island and the sinking of the torpedo boats in Operation Escort. My intimate familiarity with the Shayetet led me to the conclusion that it was capable of contending with a target as complicated as Hurgada, so long as we duly prepared for the challenges that this sort of operation entails. However, none other than the Shayetet's contemporaneous commander objected to my view.

An S-13 operation ("model") at Hurgada—Rubber crafts parachuted into the sea.

Deployment in the Red Sea Theater before the War

The aforementioned balance of power in the region left us with no choice but to operate according to von Clausewitz's known principle: the best defense is a good offense. Consequently, Red Sea Theater Headquarters' operative policy was to strike the enemy's anchorages or other targets in the vicinity of the Egyptian coast, including those that the enemy couldn't possibly have fathomed that we would dare to infiltrate, much less attack.

Accordingly, our target list could essentially be divided into two: 1) To attack Egyptian naval traffic in the Gulf of Suez with *Dabour* boats. We had already practiced this sort of operation throughout the entire year that preceded the Yom Kippur War. 2) To raid Hurgada, a mission that we had yet to train for at all. We assumed that assaults against these locations would force the enemy to concentrate on safeguarding its positions along the Red Sea front. By preoccupying the Egyptian forces with defensive tasks, we hoped to mitigate the pressure that they brought to bear on our troops and territory. Moreover, we hoped that this holding strategy would afford us with the freedom of action to operate, even from the inferior position that we found

An S-13 operation ("model") at Hurgada—Mark V rubber craft and *Snunit.*

ourselves in. Put differently, in the absence of our own missile boats in the Red Sea combat zone, the only way that the theater could fulfill its principal duty—that is, the landing of the armored division—was to launch an attack on the Hurgada Anchorage.

On August 23, 1973, about a month and a half before the war, I took part in the presentation of the Shayetet's operational plans before the admiral of the Navy, Binyamin Telem ("Bini"). The commander of the S-13, Commander Shaul Ziv, objected to attacking Hurgada so long as the advanced model of the pig, which was designed to reach and surreptitiously penetrate remote and difficult targets such as Hurgada, was not available.[7] In Ziv's estimation, the mission could not possibly succeed without the new pig, and the admiral accepted his view. Moreover, the latter turned down my suggestion to conduct an operational patrol at the target or, at the very least, draw up model exercises for the purpose of evaluating the proposal.

The Yom Kippur War

The fighting in the Red Sea Theater and *Merchav Shlomo* broke out at 1400 on October 6, 1973, as part of the general offensive that Egypt launched against Israel. All of the Egyptian army's corps took part in the massive attack: manifold raids on Sharm al-Sheikh by, among others, troops that had reached the Sinai on helicopter; attempts to ferry and land forces along the length of the Gulf of Suez's east coast and in Sharm al-Sheikh; and a southward advance on the part of forces from the Egyptian III Army that were deployed to the south of the canal. This multi-corps and far-ranging offensive testified to the fact that Egypt intended on wresting control over the southern Sinai and the surrounding maritime expanses, including the region's strategic and economic assets.

The Egyptians waged the following aerial actions along the Red Sea front:

- Twenty-eight Egyptian MIGs raided Sharm al-Sheikh. The MIGs inflicted damage on the IDF's Hawk batteries, the Ophirah Airport's takeoff path, and the communication installations in the area. That said, six of the MIGs were bagged by the IAF's two Phantom jets, which took off in their direction before the runway was bombarded. In addition, a seventh MIG was downed by antiaircraft fire from war boats and the Navy base along Sharm al-Sheikh's coastline in the Bay of Shlomo.
- Two Kelt ARM air-to-land missiles (carrying 850 kg of high explosives) took out the IAF's radar installations on top of Tsafra Hill, killing five IAF soldiers in the process.

■ Twenty-four Egyptian helicopters traversed the Gulf of Suez and dropped about 540 commandos along the Sinai coast. During the landing, eight Mil MI-8 helicopters were downed by IAF Mirages. Eventually, all 540 Egyptian commandos were either liquidated or captured by IDF units in the area, among them the 35th (Paratrooper) Brigade, which had arrived in *Merchav Shlomo* en route to the Canal Zone.

The naval dimension of the Egyptian offensive included the following actions. Two Egyptian missile boats launched four Styx missiles at the five landing craft patrolling the area between Sharm al-Sheikh and Ras Muhammad. The two Phantoms engaged the enemy boats even before they got within striking range of the landing crafts, but failed to destroy the assailants or keep them at bay. Thanks to an order that was issued in advance of the attack, the IDF crafts managed to evade the Styx missiles by landing on the riffs (a procedure that the crews drilled on a regular basis).

Rubber crafts carrying Egyptian commandos sought to land at Sharm al-Sheikh and capture the base, but were repulsed by *Dabour* boats. However, the *Dabours* lacked the velocity to overtake and damage the Egyptian crafts.

An Egyptian submarine fired three torpedoes at an Israeli tanker, which was on its way to Eilat with a full supply of oil. However, the torpedoes were off the mark and the tanker made it to Eilat unscathed. Egyptian naval forces also attempted to blockade the Red Sea and deny entry to Israeli merchant ships. An Israeli tanker and another Eilat-bound tanker that happened to be passing through this swath of sea when hostilities broke out fortunately did not run into Egyptian forces and safely reached their destinations.

An enemy minelayer mined the Strait of Jubal at the entrance to the Gulf of Suez. However, this measure only came to our attention after the war, for during the campaign itself we qualified and made use of an alternative outlet that passed through the Milan Pass, which is closer to the Sinai coast.

Elements of the above-noted Egyptian III Army sought to make their way across land from the southern section of the Suez Canal down to *Merchav Shlomo* via the coastal axis. However the continued presence of the IDF's Hawk batteries in Ras Sudr prevented the Egyptian Air Force from providing their ground forces with air cover. As a result, the 35th Brigade was able to engage the III Army's troops under the aegis of Hawk missiles and repel the invasion.

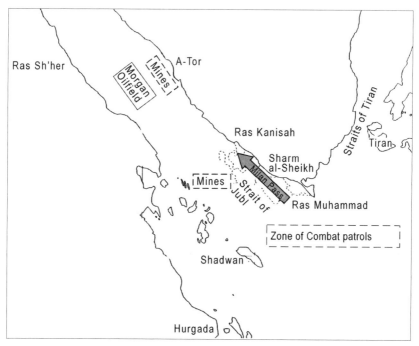

Maritime mine fields and combat patrols.

The Egyptian commandos who had infiltrated the Sinai coast on helicopters sought to establish a beachhead, and the Egyptian command was planning to bolster its grip by ferrying troops across the Gulf of Suez on board the above-mentioned seventy fishing boats. However, on the first night of the war, two *Dabour* boats attacked the Marsa T'lmet Anchorage and inflicted damage on a force of Egyptian naval commandos that was slated to preside over the crossing, and thereby managed to jumble the Egyptian invasion. Two nights later, *Dabours* sank an Egyptian De Castro boat off the shore of Ras Sudr. This action enabled the IDF to keep the Hawk missiles at Ras Sudr throughout the critical first five days of the campaign.

THE DEBATE OVER THE RED SEA THEATER'S RESPONSE TO THE EGYPTIAN OFFENSIVE

In light of the massive Egyptian offensive, the Red Sea Theater Headquarters was compelled to come up with immediate and unconventional means for extricating ourselves from the enemy's stranglehold. I demanded that the S-13 be brought to the Red Sea front at once and placed under my command. As per my request, the Shayetet's *lochamim* were in Sharm al-Sheikh by the third day of the war. Having served as their commander only two years earlier, I was well acquainted with most of the men.

The force was accompanied to Sharm al-Sheikh by the commander of the Shayetet, Commander Shaul Ziv, who appointed Lieutenant Ilan Egozi to serve as the unit's liaison and planning officer at Red Sea Theater Headquarters. Two former commanders of the Navy, Rear Admiral (Res.) Yochai Ben-Nun and Rear Admiral (Res.) Avraham Botzer ("Cheetah"), asked to contribute to the war effort by assuming auxiliary and/or advisory positions, and I agreed to their offer.

All the new arrivals were convened along with the regular headquarter staff for a meeting in which I surveyed all the major events that had transpired during the first 72 hours of the war. I emphasized the fact that Egypt's objective seemed to be quite evident: capturing Sharm al-Sheikh and the rest of *Merchav Shlomo*, along with all the region's essential installations and strategic areas. Therefore, it was imperative that we come up with a plan to stem the tide and subsequently keep the Egyptians on the defensive. I adamantly contended that the only possible way to prevent the southern Sinai "from falling into the enemy's hands like ripe fruit," was by launching an attack on the Hurgada Anchorage in order to keep the Egyptians preoccupied with defending themselves against IDF raids. However, I encountered stiff opposition from some of the meeting's most senior participants. Shaul Ziv claimed that an assault on Hurgada constituted too great a risk. In spite of all the seemingly fateful developments in the area during the first three days of the war, Ziv didn't see any reason to alter his stance from August, when the plan was originally presented to Rear Admiral Binyamin Telem. Ben-Nun shared Ziv's sentiments, while Cheetah even claimed that I had "gone over the edge" and said that he would advise the admiral to reject my idea.

My colleagues' critical response left me in stunned disbelief. I countered that Cheetah and his supporters were misreading the map and still fighting the previous war. After the meeting, Shaul Ziv returned to the north and that was the last I would see of him until the end of the war.

I left my office in a fit of rage and looked for Lieutenant Gadi Kroll, who remained in Sharm al-Sheikh to command the S-13's combat force. I told him that I was on my way to call the admiral in order to get him to approve the Shayetet's attack on Hurgada, despite the fact that his commander, Shaul Ziv, who had already left the base, objected to the plan. "If it was possible," I said, "I would personally set out with the assault force, but the present circumstances and my duties as commander of the theater prevent me from taking part in the raid. The Egyptians," I continued, "intend upon capturing *Merchav Shlomo* and aren't far from realizing their goal. Therefore, there is no better moment than now for the Shayetet to justify its existence. I know you well and am convinced that you can get the job done." Lastly, I told Gadi that it would make it easier for me to persuade the admiral to give us the green light if I could tell him that Gadi was willing to execute the mission. I then asked for his approval knowing that if he turned me down, I would have no choice but to throw in the towel and abandon the idea of attacking Hurgada. Gadi was well aware of the difficulties that he was up against, but nevertheless responded, "We'll do it!"

I rang up the admiral, and his deputy, Rear Admiral Tzvi Tirosh ("Hershel"), took the call. Tirosh told me that Rear Admiral Telem had given him instructions to approve whatever I suggested, but that I should bear in mind the fact that there would be no air support whatsoever. With that, we were on our way.

DIFFICULTIES ATTACKING HURGADA

Sharm al-Sheikh is over sixty miles from Hurgada as the crow flies. At the time, this was an enormous distance for the Shayetet's light vehicles (primarily Mark V rubber crafts and *Snuniyot*) to traverse, especially considering the choppy seas that they were likely to encounter. What's more, given the lack of sites or signposts along the way,[8] we would have to make do with rudimentary navigation throughout the length of the journey.

We would have to avail ourselves of the S-13's above-surface vehicles, which were liable to be detected at any stage of the mission. On account of the long distance involved, part of the journey would have to be made in broad daylight (either on the way to or back from the target). In addition, the troops would not be able to draw on either air or naval support.

The layout and defenses of the Hurgada Anchorage were also riddled with obstacles. The main entrance to the anchorage was about two miles north of

Location of target and zone of operation (fifty-five nautical miles from Sharm al-Sheikh).

the actual target, namely the pier along which the boats were berthed. On the one hand, this was quite a distance for a foot diver; on the other hand, surface crafts would be continuously exposed to lookout posts on both sides of the ingress and within the anchorage itself. The anchorage's southern entrance was only about a mile from the pier. However, the passage was narrow, so that divers—not to mention surface crafts—ran the risk of being spotted. What's more, the route was teeming with coral reefs, which were liable to ensnare, if not disable, the boats' propellers. The defenders frequently scattered depth

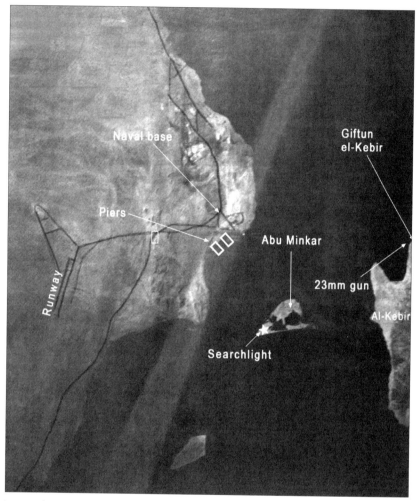

Layout of target.

charges against divers along the length of the coastline, particularly next to the piers.

Since Hurgada's harbor was cut off from the rest of the sea by the Gifton Shoal, its waters were tranquil and highly transparent. As a result, submerged objects could be spotted at considerable depths from the surface-level observation posts. The coral reefs in the area extend quite a distance from the coast (nearly 1,100 yards at certain points). During high tide, the reef is covered in water that conceals its borders, so that our boats were liable to scrape against the coral or get entangled in the reef.

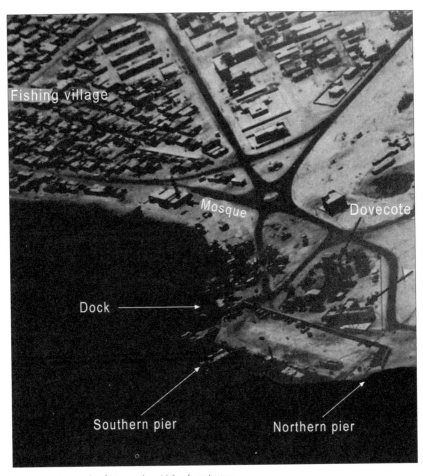

Aerial photograph of Hurgada—Wharf and piers.

Small cannons and light weapons were dispersed throughout the anchorage: on either bank, the beach, Gifton Shoal, and boats. The anchorage is shaped like a long "bottleneck" and is thus exposed to the whims of the prevailing northerly winds. This layout causes a "nostril effect" that accelerates the pace of Hurgada's currents. In addition, the currents are influenced by the movement of the high and low tides, which alternate every couple of hours. These conditions were likely to impede the progress of swimmers and divers alike.

From my experience in the War of Attrition, I knew that all these obstacles could be surmounted by engendering the right conditions for catching the enemy off guard. The shock of such a blow would blunt the defenders' instincts and preoccupy them with "licking their wounds." Consequently, even if there were favorable circumstances for chasing down the Shayetet's commandos, the latter would be able to slip away from the target on their small and nimble crafts. During the briefings, I reiterated this important point to the *lochamim* time and again.

The First Operation at Hurgada

Two pairs of divers and another backup diver (some of whom were on reserve duty) were chosen for the first mission. After getting within striking range, on board three Mark V rubber crafts, the commandos would submerge and penetrate the Hurgada Anchorage, where they would endeavor to plant limpet mines on military targets, preferably missile boats. The men were given express orders not to damage civilian crafts.

According to the plan, the rubber crafts were to reach the entrance of the anchorage, hug the western coastline, and then drop off the divers near an Egyptian naval camp in the vicinity of the piers. The boats were also charged with picking up the divers at the end of the mission from the same location. In addition, another rubber craft would be placed at the disposal of a technical backup force. The reserve craft would be mounted on the deck of one of the two *Dabour* boats, which were instructed to wait along the coast of Ras Muhammad (a small salient on the southern tip of the Sinai Peninsula) in order to defend the force against maritime intervention and provide radar warning.

Lieutenant Gadi Kroll and Lieutenant Commander Eli Marek were chosen to command the divers and the rubber boats, respectively. Boat #1 included the pair of divers Gadi Kroll and Petty Officer First Class Dan Uzieli, and its operators were Eli Marek, Chief Petty Officer (Res.) Itamar Levi, and Petty Officer First Class Udi Grossman. Boat #2 contained the diving tandem of First Lieutenant (Res.) Amnon Shani and Petty Officer First Class Yaron Matzliach and was operated by Chief Petty Officer (Res.) David Kliot and Petty Officer First Class Uri Stein. The backup diver, Petty Officer First Class (Res.) Avinoam Brakin, and Mark V operators, Petty Officer First Class Yossi Gozni and Petty Officer First Class Ran Nir, were on boat #3. Lastly, boat #4 was assigned to the technical backup force and was operated by Lieutenant (Res.) Israel Dagai and Petty Officer First Class Reuven Spitzer.

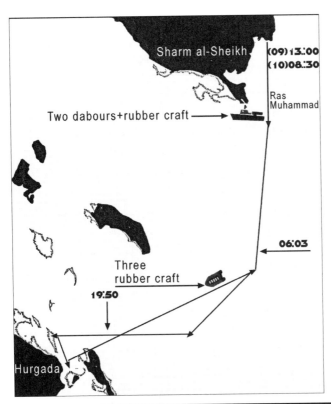

Operation *Magbit* 10—First attack (night of October 9–10, 1973), carried out by divers.

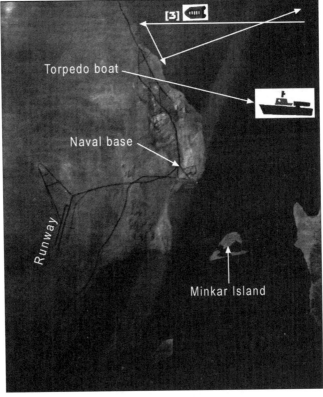

THE OPERATION

On October 9, the force set out for Hurgada at 1300 and encountered rough seas. The crews conducted a test run off the coast of Ras Muhammad. Although the sputtering motors were replaced with the ones on the reserve boat, the force continued to have engine problems along the way. At 1950, the force reached the northern tip of the Giftun Shoal, whereupon it turned westward toward the reef lining Hurgada's coastline. The force then continued southward as the boats scraped the floor of the beach. There were three reasons for "scraping" along the coast: the boats blended in with the coastline and were less prominent than they would have been had they proceeded on top of the reef table; the proximity to the shore helped them gain their bearings and identify targets; and we assumed that the currents would be weaker by the coast.

At 2220, after two and a half hours of stealthy yet slow progress along the coast, the commandos identified the profile of a torpedo boat as well as people moving about on the shore. The force thus realized that it was within striking range and started getting ready to lower the divers into the water. For a moment, they considered dropping the divers by the adjacent reef, next to Minkar Island, some 1,300 yards from the pier. However, they ultimately decided to stick with the dipping point near the Egyptian mainland, primarily due to the fear of stronger currents away from the shore. The boats thus continued their methodical southerly advance along the coast. Soon after, one of the propellers rammed into a couple of rocks, creating some noise. The men correspondingly noticed a maritime vessel heading in their direction from the south. Consequently, the force turned east and then north toward Giftun, at the same slow pace, in order to evade the enemy boat, while keeping track of its movement. The Mark Vs then entered the channel between Giftun and Minkar, where they laid low for ninety minutes or so.

At this stage, a report came into the command post about an Egyptian torpedo boat at the entrance to the anchorage, which was preventing the force from reaching the dipping point. I notified the combatants that if the torpedo boat didn't take off by 0200, they were to return to base for the following reasons. The force was already two hours behind schedule. Given the swimming/diving distance between the troops' present location and the target, if we would have proceeded with the mission, the force would have to execute the withdrawal and collection phases after the break of dawn, thereby losing the cover of darkness. The boats were instructed to wait for the divers to return with their motors running. Therefore, if the force stayed past the designated hour, they would not have enough fuel for the return trip to Sharm al-Sheikh. (In fact, it turned out that all they had left were four tanks of fuel.)

In the end, the torpedo boat did not budge and the crews were forced to withdraw. On its way back, the force indeed ran out of gas about 5.5 nautical miles south of Ras Muhammad. I thus ordered the *Dabour* boat that was carrying the backup craft to set out in the force's direction and refuel the Mark Vs. At 0830 the next morning, after twenty hours at sea, the combat team finally made it back to Sharm al-Sheikh.

After the mission, the admiral of the Navy criticized me for risking a *Dabour* by allowing it to enter the missile-defended zone. "Under no circumstances," I replied, "were we going to abandon the *lochamim* who ran out of fuel!"

The debriefing of the first operation at Hurgada led to the following conclusions:

- The mission proved that it was possible to safely navigate through the missile-defended zone and make it to the target and back without being detected.
- After reexamining the air photos and maps, we realized that the rubber crafts had penetrated farther than planned. Nevertheless, they were in position to lower the divers into the sea. This indicated that the installation's defenders were not on high alert.
- The Egyptians were clearly unaware of the fact that we were at the target, so that the element of surprise was still intact.
- Despite the advantage that was gained from familiarizing ourselves with the target, there was still room to improve our knowledge and the manner in which we prepared the boats.

We decided to re-embark on the mission a mere twenty-four hours later. However, this time around we would not dispatch a backup diver and the third boat would be designated exclusively for the transport of additional tanks of fuel. What's more, we decided to transfer *Snuniyot*,[9] the above-mentioned attack boats, to the theater of combat.

The Second Operation in Hurgada

The second offensive action against Hurgada was carried out on the heels of the first. In the end, the *Snuniyot* did not arrive at Sharm al-Sheikh on time, so we decided to tentatively incorporate them into the rescue phase. Although the second diving pair was replaced by Avinoam Brakin and Meir Levi, the composition of the combat command echelon and the mode of action were basically the same. The operators of the Mark V with the spare fuel tanks were Lieutenant (Res.) Israel Dagai and Chief Petty Officer (Res.) David Kliot. The two rescue *Snuniyot*, which made it on time for the withdrawal phase, were under the helm of the deputy commander of the S-13, Lieutenant Commander Gadi Sheffi. A veteran combat soldier, Chief Petty Officer Itamar Levi (Res.) was on alert along with a rescue helicopter crew at Ophira Airport. However, any airborne rescue operation would be absolutely limited to areas outside the arch of the aerial missile-defended zone.

MOVEMENT TO THE TARGET

The operation commenced at 1400 on October 11. A *Dabour* escorted the rubber crafts and combatants until the split-up point at Ras Muhammad. On account of calm seas and lack of engine trouble, the force made it to the designated area at 1500, ninety minutes ahead of schedule. From that point on, the crafts slowed down in order to avoid reaching the target in the light of day. At 1810, the force reached a position southeast of Shadwan Island, which was out of the island's radar range. They then turned west and set a course for the coral reef at Hurgada. Along the way, the rubber crafts stopped to refuel with the help of their "mini-tanker," the third Mark V, whereupon the force headed southward, scraping the surface until they identified the anchorage's "fuel pier."

At 2030, the divers were ready to exit the boats. Since the force arrived a half hour earlier than planned, the commandos decided to enter the water some 550 yards north of the planned dipping point, for the purpose of minimizing the chances of detection on account of the full moon, or getting stuck on the reef. Once the divers had departed, the boats drew to within about

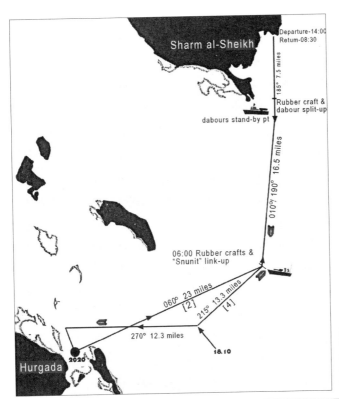

Sharm al-Sheikh

Departure-14:00
Return-08:30

185° 7.5 miles

Rubber craft &
dabour split-up

dabours stand-by pt

010° 190° 16.5 miles

06:00 Rubber crafts &
"Snunit" link-up

060° 23 miles
[2]

215° 13.3 miles
[4]

270° 12.3 miles

18.10

2020°

Hurgada

Second attack (night of
October 11–12), carried
out by divers—Surprise
attained by both location
and method.

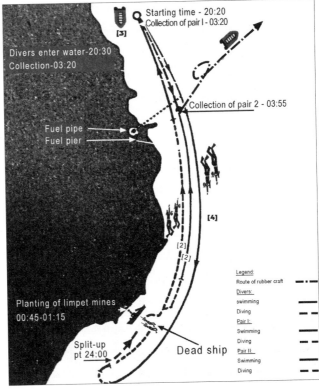

Starting time - 20:20
Collection of pair I - 03:20

[3]

Divers enter water-20:30
Collection-03:20

Collection of pair 2 - 03:55

Fuel pipe
Fuel pier

[4]

[2]
[2]

Planting of limpet mines
00:45-01:15

Split-up
pt 24:00

Dead ship

Legend:
Route of rubber craft
Divers:
swimming
Diving
Pair I:
Swimming
Diving
Pair II:
Swimming
Diving

250 yards of the coast, so as not to stand out. They set anchor opposite the Egyptian naval camp, but the crews were prepared to detach on a moment's notice.

Meanwhile, the four frogmen began to swim toward the targets. However, their progress was slow because of the strong currents and the blasts from depth charges, which Egyptian defenders were throwing into the water every minute or so. The divers accidentally passed the anchorage and had to hook a strong left in the direction of the coast, while submerged in a company formation, before "scraping" back to the north.

At 2330, three hours after entering the water, the four divers, under the command of Gadi Kroll, rose to the surface and continued to swim northward, scraping the coast until they were near the epicenter of the explosions. By that point, they could make out the boats and thus realized that they were close to the pier and the targets. A half hour later, Gadi ordered his men to get ready for the final approach to the pier and warned them to only attack military targets.

As planned, the divers split up into two pairs. The first tandem—Lieutenant Gadi Kroll and Petty Officer First Class Dan Uzieli—dove northward and then eastward, before approaching the southern pier via a perpendicular route. After ten minutes of diving, they rose to the surface and noticed several fishing boats as well as a large dark craft. Gadi and Dan dove toward the latter, but realized that it was a civilian craft. They then spanned the length of the boat, until they reached its bow, whereupon the two frogmen surfaced and surveyed the area for about ten minutes, under cover of the large hulk. Throughout that time, they heard explosions and could feel the strong subaqueous blasts, but there were no targets to be found. Gadi thus decided to dive toward the area in which the Egyptians were setting off the most charges, under the assumption that they would find a target there. Along the way, Gadi rose for a peek and realized that he was at the center of the anchorage. During a lull between the explosions, Gadi and Uzieli identified a maritime vessel that, from a distance, appeared to be a missile or torpedo boat and headed off in its direction.

Once they were beneath the target, the pair confirmed that it was indeed a missile boat, on account of the four axes beneath its stern, and started planting the limpet mines. They initially had slight difficulty sticking the devices on the surface, but eventually affixed four mines and anti-removal systems. The demolition action was over by 0115. Since no other targets were spotted and time was running out, the diving tandem was forced to return to the Mark Vs. On their way back, Gadi and Dan encountered a plethora of exploding charges, which were being tossed from Egyptian rubber boats circling about the anchorage. The sheer volume of the blasts aroused suspicion that they had been detected. Consequently, the two divers plunged to a great depth—a dangerous move in its own right—before proceeding northwards. About fifty minutes later, at around 0200, they reached the vicinity of the fuel pier, and Gadi reported that his pair had completed its part of the mission. At 0320, the rubber crafts linked up with the first pair of divers, who were utterly exhausted.

After the divers had split up, the second pair, Petty Officer First Class (Res.) Avinoam Brakin and Petty Officer First Class Meir Levi, dove in the direction of the southern pier for about a half hour. Upon reaching their destination, they spotted a few shipping vessels along the pier, but did not identify any military targets. While evading the subaqueous blasts, Meir's life vest suddenly filled up, perhaps due to an unintentional movement, and he was unable to remain submerged. Correspondingly, the pair sighted the Egyptian rubber boat that was tossing charges into the water. As a result, the frogmen decided to withdraw from the anchorage and return to the rubber crafts. In the meantime, the three boats and the first diving tandem, Gadi Kroll and Dan Uzieli, had already reached the collection point, where they waited for Avinoam and Meir to return.

At 0340, the troops at the collection point spotted the "missing pair's" identification lamp as well as people bustling about on the beach. The robust activity aroused their suspicion that the Egyptians were on to something. Consequently, the boats raised anchor and paddled away, until they were about one thousand yards from the coast. The crews then started their engines, turned southward, and entered the anchorage in order to retrieve Avinoam and Meir, who were located about forty yards from the tip of the fuel pier.

After picking up Avinoam and Meir—who were also on their last legs— the three Mark Vs headed off toward Giftun Shoal, picking up speed. This apparently stirred up a bit of noise, for the force soon came under heavy fire from the direction of the coast, expediting its departure from the anchorage.

After putting another one thousand yards behind them, the fire from the shore came to a halt. At this point, Chief Petty Officer Yossi Gozni and Chief Petty Officer Ran Nir's boat started to lag behind the others due to a problem with one of their engines, and they were unable to get it restarted. The other two boats turned in their tracks and returned to the third craft, but their boosts failed to get the engine going. In consequence, the force abandoned the laggard craft and its men were transferred to the other Mark Vs, before resuming the journey back to Sharm al-Sheikh.

At this stage, a report came in to the command post from Lieutenant Commander Eli Marek about some sort of encounter. Eli's tone of voice sounded rather panicky and he asked us to organize air support, but did not provide any further details. Although two *Snuniyot*, under the command of the Shayetet's deputy commander, were out in the field and ready to lend a hand, I put in a request for air support. IAF planes subsequently took off and created a diversion by setting off illumination flares (outside the missile-defended zone, of course). Meanwhile, I patiently waited for another report and resisted the temptation of contacting the force, as I did not want to break the "wireless silence." However, after twenty minutes had passed without a word, I picked up the speaker and contacted Eli Marek. He responded that the force was on its way back and was neither being pursued nor fired upon by the enemy. In addition, Eli informed me that mines were planted on an Egyptian missile boat.

The returning force met up with the *Snuniyot* at 0600, but the Mark Vs continued to proceed without assistance. By 0830, all our troops were back in Sharm al-Sheikh.

The mines that Gadi and Dan planted subsequently detonated and sunk the Egyptian missile boat. On account of the craft's wooden hull, only the stern capsized and the bow continued to jut out of the water. By dint of the element of surprise, both with respect to the location and method, our forces returned from the mission unscathed. Gadi Kroll conducted himself in an exemplary fashion and was decorated with the Gallantry Medal. This was Gadi's second citation, as he was also awarded the Distinguished Service Medal for his role in the assault on Green Island.

On the same night as the second attack on Hurgada (October 11–12), the Egyptians waged another attack on Sharm al-Sheikh. Four enemy rubber crafts approached the port while launching RPG rockets, but they were turned aside by two *Dabour* boats before Egyptian commandos even managed to step foot on shore. However, the *Dabours* lacked the necessary speed to intercept the Egyptian crafts. Shortly after (according to estimates), on October 12–13 the Egyptians mined the swath of sea off A-Tor, between the Morgan Oil field and the coast. However, none of our troops was injured by the mines, apparently due to the sparseness of the field.

On October 14, the SOP for Operation Ohr Yarok, the landing of the armored division, got under way. The following evening a pair of enemy missile boats launched four missiles from the vicinity of Shadwan Island at radar reflectors, which we had staked onto a reef by the Strait of Milan before the war, in order to mark the pass. Apparently, the enemy mistook the reflectors for maritime vessels. In any event, the incident testified to the fact that the Egyptian missile threat on the entrance to the Gulf of Suez was still in effect. This action, along with the other incidents that transpired during the previous few days, indicated that we had yet to attain the freedom of action necessary for launching Ohr Yarok, and the armored landing was ultimately scrapped.

On October 18, the admiral of the Navy, Binyamin Telem, came to the theater for the first time since the war broke out. I took advantage of his visit to convince him of the need to launch another offensive action on Hurgada. During our meeting, I averred that this sort of a raid would buttress the impact of the first attack. Moreover, the IDF had to retaliate for the subsequent Egyptian missile attacks in the entrance to the Gulf of Suez. I proposed that we utilize *Patzchanim*, new explosive boats that the S-13 had recently transferred to Sharm al-Sheikh, which would enable us to surprise the enemy both with respect to the timing and means.

The *Patzchan* consisted of the hull of a *Snunit* with 270 kg of high explosives packed into its bow. The *Snunit's* reliable hull enabled it to ply through stormy seas. With this in mind, we began to develop the new *Patzchan* class of explosive boats immediately following the Green Island Raid. The weapon worked in the following fashion: the boat's operator would storm the target, lock in on it, and then eject from the craft by sliding the seat backward along a track that was assembled on the stern's deck. As the boat itself continued to rush toward the target, the operator would be left floating in the water. Upon impact the unmanned *Patzchan* would set off a massive explosion. The

Patzchan.

development of the *Patzchan* began while I was still the S-13's commander, and two of the unit's engineers, Michael Avraham and Dani Raz, presided over the planning and construction. As soon as the war broke out, the Shayetet's technical staff spared no effort to render the *Patzchanim* operational.

In response to my proposal, Rear Admiral Telem contended that the *Patzchan* was a new system that had yet to be declared operational. I countered that even if the *Patzchanim* missed the targeted missile boats, the objective would be achieved, for this time around it was important to engender a conspicuous explosion in the anchorage. This sort of an attack, I added, would intensify the pressure that was already on the Egyptians and force them to concentrate on self-defense. As a result, the entrance to the Gulf would be unclogged and we would be able to launch Operation Ohr Yarok. The mission's objective was indeed defined along these lines, and the admiral gave us the green light, albeit with one reservation: the attack would only be carried out if there were missile boats inside the anchorage.

The Third Attack on Hurgada

The *Patzchanim*, which were designated the primary offensive means for the third operation at Hurgada, reached Sharm al-Sheikh on October 17. As soon as they arrived, the explosive boats were prepared for battle and test-driven by the Shayetet's operators. The following evening a drill was conducted on a "model" target. The exercise began at 2230 and ended the following morning at 0515. This marked the first time that such a maneuver was ever conducted with a *Patzchan*.

At the summation of the exercise, we set forth the principal techniques for the operation. We anticipated that the target would be located in a dark area alongside the pier. Therefore, before the *Patzchan* operator began his assault, the mother *Snunit's* crew would toss a hand flare at the pier from a distance of three hundred to four hundred feet, so the target was directly illuminated.

The mother *Snunit* would be charged with directing the *Patzchan*. More specifically, the *Snunit's* crew would illuminate the target and guide the *Patzchan* until it was opposite the enemy missile boat, whereupon it would clear the way for the explosive boat. The *Patzchan's* operator would then lock in on the target and begin his solo run. At a distance of about one hundred yards, the operator would eject backward in his seat via the back deck, and a parachute would shoot open in order to prevent him from gliding forward. Meanwhile, the unmanned explosive boat would continue charging the target. The conditions in the field would dictate whether the mother *Snunit* collected the ejected operator before or after the explosion.

The plan was presented to me on the morning of October 19, and I immediately gave it my approval. Given the limitations on movement and maneuverability and the risk of being detected at the southern entrance, the force would once again penetrate the anchorage from the north. The H-hour at the target was set for early morning.

Preparations were made throughout that entire day, and the admiral held a short visit with the Shayetet's commandos. Bini checked the battle readiness of the *Patzchanim*, tested the combatants' familiarity with the target, and inquired as to the expected assemblage of enemy boats in the anchorage. Intelligence sources had indeed informed us that Egyptian missile boats were moored in the harbor. At 1930, a final briefing was held in my office, and the force set out for Hurgada at 2230.

The Shayetet's deputy commander, Gadi Sheffi, stood at the head of a combat force that consisted of the following men and means:

- *Patzchan* #1 was operated by Chief Petty Officer (Res.) Yedidya Ya'ari ("Didi"), who had recovered from a serious injury at Green Island and completed his regular army service, then returned to the unit from Holland as soon as the war broke out.
- *Patzchan* #2 was operated by Chief Petty Officer (Res.) Yair Michaeli.
- Mother *Snunit* #1 was manned by Lieutenant Commander Gadi Sheffi (the force's aforementioned commander),[10] Lieutenant Commander Eli Marek, Chief Petty Officer (Res.) Itamar Levi, Petty Officer First Class Yossi Gozni, and Petty Officer First Class Uri Stein (the RPG operator).
- Mother *Snunit* #2 was manned by Amnon Shani (the commander), David Marcus, Ehud Grossman, and Dani Eitan (the RPG operator).
- The rescue *Snunit* (at Ras Muhammad) was manned by Lieutenant Gadi Kroll (the commander), Lieutenant (Res.) Israel Dagai, and Chief Petty Officer (Res.) David Kliot.
- Moshe Dotan and Giora Gottesman manned the rescue helicopter (which was restricted to actions outside of the missile-defended zone).

COMBAT AT THE TARGET

The force encountered strong waves and winds during the final two legs of the journey to the target. On account of the *Patzchan*'s elevated seating arrangement, the operators were exposed to bursts of sea water that burned their eyes. Furthermore, the intensive preparations for the mission, including the "model drill," had kept the men from getting so much as a moment of sleep over the past thirty hours. However, the navigation to the target was easier, thanks to the radars that were installed on the mother *Snuniyot* and the fact that many of the *lochamim* had already been to the anchorage during the previous two operations.

The four boats entered the anchorage along the length of the reefs, which were clearly visible in low tide, and proceeded in a column formation until they were adjacent to Minkar Island. At 0350, the men formed up some three hundred yards from the dock. Donning infrared night-vision goggles, Gadi Sheffi positively identified a civilian craft and two fishing boats tied to the southern pier. The disabled missile boat, with its capsized stern and bow pointing northward, was spotted at the northern part of the dock. Lastly, Gadi

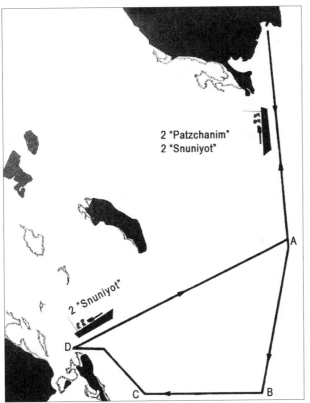

2 "Patzchanim"
2 "Snuniyot"

2 "Snuniyot"

A

D

C

B

Third attack (night of October 19–20, 1973) with *Patzchanim*—Surprise attained by means and timing.

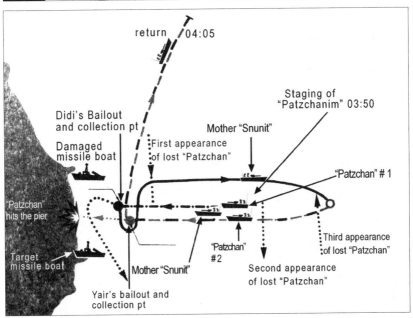

return 04:05

Staging of "Patzchanim" 03:50

Didi's Bailout and collection pt

Mother "Snunit"

First appearance of lost "Patzchan"

Damaged missile boat

"Patzchan" # 1

"Patzchan" hits the pier

Third appearance of lost "Patzchan"

"Patzchan" #2

Second appearance of lost "Patzchan"

Mother "Snunit"

Target missile boat

Yair's bailout and collection pt

identified another missile boat moored to the dock about sixty to seventy yards to his south, and he duly designated it the target of the attack.

The immediate vicinity was swarming with enemy troops. On the part of the dock between the two missile boats, there was a host of soldiers moving around four or five trucks. The assailants also heard the incessant explosions of the depth charges that the Egyptians were throwing into the harbor.

In what turned out to be an unfortunate and somewhat fateful error, Gadi did not have the *Patzchan* operators identify the targeted missile boat with his infrared goggles. Instead, he merely pointed out the direction of the target with his hand, but neither Didi, who was in *Patzchan #1*, nor Yair, who was standing next to him in *Patzchan #2*, managed to make out the missile boat. Thereafter, Gadi shouted at Didi to follow him, and the two boats stormed toward the pier, while *Patzchan #2* and mother *Snunit #2* waited in their place. The crew on board *Snunit #1* launched an illumination flare, but it plopped into the water between the charging explosive boat and the dock. Although Didi was already well into his approach, he had yet to actually distinguish the target. In addition, he advanced too close to the pier to eject, so he turned around with the intention of giving it another go. In the meantime, the errant flare had alerted the anchorage's defenders, and Didi drew heavy fire from the coast and a host of other sources.

Didi commenced his second run, but still could not make out the missile boat. He thus asked the *Snunit* to fire off another flare, while continuing to advance without pausing for the illumination. In any event, the second flare was also off the mark, so that Didi once again lacked a concrete target. Given the circumstances, the future admiral of the Navy decided to hit the southern tip of the pier, under the assumption that the *Patzchan's* potent explosive bow would damage everything in the immediate area. He locked the *Patzchan* onto the improvised target and ejected himself, while the explosive boat continued to close in on the pier. However, after one hundred yards, it suddenly veered off to the left, raced past the tip of the pier, and vanished. As Gadi's *Snunit* fished Didi out of the water, under heavy fire from the coast, the *Patzchan* darted by, coming within only ten yards.

In the meantime, the troops in the second mother *Snunit* and Yair, the operator of *Patzchan #2*, were busy watching Didi's escapades. As Didi got into position for his second approach, Yair, who had yet to identify the elusive missile boat himself, stepped off to the side in order to avoid a collision with his fellow operator and evade the fire from the shore. At the very moment that Yair identified the capsized missile boat, the "deviant" *Patzchan* flitted by.

After collecting Didi, Gadi Sheffi linked up with Yair. Upon receiving Gadi's order, Yair began to storm the port, despite being unable to locate the targeted missile boat. He informed Gadi of his predicament, but the latter instructed him to proceed on his wing and promised him illumination. Yair activated the mechanisms and began his approach. However, the flare that Gadi launched touched down about 250 yards shy of the pier and instantly became an aiming point for three guns on the coast. Yair hooked a sharp left in order to avert the incoming fire, but took a couple of hits to the bow and stern. He then straightened up opposite the line of fire and charged the southern section of the dock. By this point, Yair could make out the pier, but not the targeted missile boat; Yair subsequently ejected himself from the *Patzchan* at a distance of about one hundred yards from his replacement target. The explosive boat barreled into the pier and blew it up, bringing the gunfire from that direction to an abrupt halt.

Thereafter, Gadi set off another flare, which inadvertently exposed Yair to the gunners on the adjacent pier. When the illumination fizzled out, Gadi's *Snunit* sailed over to Yair and pulled him onto the boat. The entire force then turned northward toward the exit of the anchorage. After distancing themselves about a mile north of the pier, the troops saw the "aberrant" *Patzchan* go up in flames with a loud bang in the area between Minkar Island and the pier.

The assailants made it out of the anchorage, but the Egyptian fire and illumination persisted for another fifteen to twenty minutes. At this stage, the *Snuniyot* began to encounter intermittent engine problems, and the boats resorted to tugging one another until finally reaching Sharm al-Sheikh at 0900.

Though damaged by fragments, the Egyptian missile boat was not eliminated. Had the *Patzchanim*'s operators observed the targets with the night-vision equipment before they commenced their attack, the missile boat may very well have been destroyed. In any event, the pier was ruined and the commandos' adherence to the mission and their bravery were indeed worthy of praise! Nevertheless, the *lochamim* returned to base in a disappointed mood, but from my vantage point, as the theater's commander, the primary stated objective—to effect an explosion within the boundaries of the anchorage—was attained, even if "only" the pier, and not the missile boat, was destroyed. In fact, intelligence interceptions of enemy communications pointed to the fact that the Egyptians were in a state of panic—chasing ghosts and toiling to reinforce the anchorage's defenses.

The Fourth Attack on Hurgada

Upon returning from the third offensive action against Hurgada, the commandos were informed that they were to fly back to the north that same afternoon (October 20). While the commandos were on the ramp of the plane, I received a call from Rear Admiral "Bini" Telem, who informed me that Operation Ohr Yarok was back on the agenda. In the run-up to the armored landing, the admiral wanted us to launch another attack on Hurgada. This marked the first time that the initiative for an assault against Hurgada came from the side of the admiral. Telem also informed me that Light Assault Weapons (LAW) antitank rockets had arrived on the "air train" from the United States[11] and that he wanted the Shayetet to infiltrate Hurgada with *Snuniyot* and destroy a missile boat with the new weapons. Bini promised that twenty LAW rockets would arrive in Sharm al-Sheikh the next morning, along with instructors who would teach us how to operate them.

I told the admiral that if an additional attack on Hurgada was essential to attaining the freedom of movement for Ohr Yarok, then we would carry out the mission. However, I added that in my estimation his proposed method of operation significantly reduced the chances of success. Therefore, I would have to personally preside over the mission and accompany the force to the target. The admiral approved of my request on the spot.

As soon as I got off the phone, I rushed to pluck the soldiers off the plane. They appeared awe-stricken and had a difficult time digesting the intentions of the senior brass. I then called up Gadi Sheffi and informed him of the mission and its objective, as well as the method and timetables involved. I let him know that I would personally command the mission and join the commandos in the field. In addition, I asked him to bring all the details to the attention of his men. Naturally, I was also concerned that Gadi, who had served as my deputy when I was the commander of the Shayetet, would feel as if I was doubting his ability to lead. For this very reason, I made it a point to eluci-

date the division of responsibilities, according to which I would preside over the operation and he would command the force. I added that conditions at the target and the mode of operation—dictated to us from above—required immediate reactions and decisions, which were critical to the mission's success. Therefore, instead of giving him orders from the command post in Sharm al-Sheikh, we would both occupy the same *Snunit*. I would set policy and assume responsibility for the decisions—just as I would have done from the command post—while Gadi would command the force.

Above all, my insistence on setting out to sea and penetrating the target together with the *lochamim* stemmed from reasons of morale. I had to dispel the notion that "they are sending us on a suicide mission." As the one who initiated the three previous actions at Hurgada, I felt a deep sense of responsibility for the safety of the troops and wanted to be with them on the front line. Finally, on account of my personal experience and strong bond with most of the men from my days as their commander in the Shayetet, I felt that it was essential for me to head out with the *lochamim* and orchestrate the operation from the field, especially considering the fact that the circumstances surrounding this particular mission were more complex than ever before.

Gadi Sheffi understood and accepted my position. He asked that I allow the troops, who had just returned from the previous mission in the morning, to relax and get in a full night's sleep. I consented, for I also knew that the rockets would only be arriving the following morning, but I asked that they get to work on the three *Snuniyot* at once. Moreover, I told Gadi that I was planning to set the H-hour for 0400, a mere one hour before the break of dawn, in order to ensure that we caught the enemy off guard. This schedule enabled us to devote the entire next day and the beginning of that evening to preparations, study, and drills, before embarking on the mission that same night.

As already alluded to, the assignment was replete with dangerous obstacles. On two occasions, the Egyptians bore witness to the fact that we were capable of penetrating the anchorage. Therefore, the enemy was probably going to be on red alert. We were planning to infiltrate the very heart of the anchorage with two surface crafts. Under the circumstances, we could expect to be detected and exposed to heavy fire—the magnitude of which we had already encountered during the two previous operations—from manifold sources. The force had no previous experience with the weapon it was slated

Shayetet 13 at Hurgada during the Yom Kippur War, Operation *Magbit* 16 fourth attack (night of October 21–22, 1973)—Surprise attained by method, means, and timing.

to use. We were unaware of the LAW's effectiveness or even its range, and the rockets would have to be launched from a teetering boat.

To top it all off, I was tormented by the prospects of the missile "nightmare" that would await the troops who were assigned to carry out Operation Ohr Yarok should we fail to fulfill the mission's objectives. We knew the terrible tragedy that a lone Styx missile could inflict on our landing crafts (such as the INS *Bat-Sheva*), which were slated to transport the tanks and *shiryonerim* (members of the Armored Corps) across the Gulf of Suez.

PLANNING THE OPERATION

The limited stock of twenty LAW rockets would have to suffice for both the exercises and the operation. With this in mind, we decided to handle the entire question of weapons in the following manner: ten rockets would be allocated to the exercises (five per boat) and ten to the operation itself (five per boat); only one commando in each *Snunit* would be trained to serve as the crew's "sniper"; and in the event that we failed to hit the target with any of the rockets, each boat would also be equipped with a Gur combat charge (28 kg of high explosives). The Gur would be manually thrown onto the deck of the missile boat from short range. Moreover, the charge could be used to detonate a *Snunit* should we be forced to abandon ship.

Upon receiving the LAWs, we didn't know the appropriate range at which to fire the rockets from the *Snunit*. On the one hand, we had to be close enough to the targeted missile boat in order to hit it. On the other hand, if we fired from too close a distance, we would be susceptible to fire from the boat's crew. Likewise, if the LAW accidentally hit, or even came close to, one of the warheads of the missiles on the target's deck (each of which packed a ton of high explosives), the subsequent blast was liable to catapult us "into the heavens," along with the missile boat. Therefore, we spent the morning of October 21 out at sea launching LAW rockets at maritime targets and concluded that the maximum range was 110 yards. During a briefing that was held after the exercise, we decided that, since the actual attack would be taking place in the dark of night, another practice session would be held in the early evening, once it was dark, for the purpose of determining the final launching range. In addition, I instructed the troops not to fire the MAGs on either side of the bow without my express permission, for they contained tracers that could be exploited as aim points for enemy fire. In contrast, rocket fire generates a flash that instantly fades away.

Once again, the anchorage was to be infiltrated from the northern point of ingress. After the previous two assaults from the north, I was convinced that the Egyptians would be waiting for us at the southern portal.

Rear Admiral (Res.) Yochai Ben-Nun, who arrived at front as an adviser, claimed that I should not accompany the force to the target on the grounds that no one else was as well versed as I was in the nuts and bolts of Operation Ohr Yarok, which was slated to be executed soon after the mission at hand. I replied that, "If I don't go to Hurgada, there won't be an Ohr Yarok either." Moreover, I contended that both my deputy and the Operations Directorate's officer in the Red Sea Theater were also up-to-date on all the details of the mission.

This time around Yochai, who was originally opposed to attacking Hurgada, tried to pressure me into letting him take part in the combat. Although I didn't feel that this was a prudent step, I left the matter to the discretion of the admiral of the Navy, who cleared Yochai's request. It was agreed that Yochai

Komar missile boat.

would command the rescue/technical backup force on board the third *Snunit*, which would remain at the entrance to the harbor.

FINAL PREPARATIONS

At 1700 on October 21, the force was given a detailed briefing in my bureau. The meeting was also attended by the headquarters' staff and Ilan Egozi (the Shayetet's liaison officer). A half hour into the meeting, I suddenly received word from Navy Headquarters that the operation had been cancelled, without any explanation whatsoever. I immediately tried to get the admiral of the Navy on the line. After repeated efforts, the Corps' deputy commander, Tzvi Tirosh, finally deigned to take my call and I demanded an explanation. Much to my bewilderment, Tirosh told me that the operation was cancelled on account of our request for air support. I responded that not only was no such request submitted, but we refuse to accept that sort of assistance. "Since our first conversation at the beginning of the war," I continued, "I have been well aware of the fact that the Air Force cannot enter the boundaries of the missile-defended zone." Five minutes later, clearance was renewed.

During that same briefing, the chief of the Navy's Intelligence Department informed me that a searchlight would be operated by Egyptian artillery soldiers at the entrance to the anchorage. I asked him at which entrance, north or south, but he replied that they didn't know. I shared this bit of information with the soldiers and added that the searchlight would actually help us, for it would betray the defenders' position. In light of this development, a final decision over which entrance to use would be taken out in the field, once the combat force had confirmed the location of the searchlight.

We subsequently conducted the planned evening exercise, which lasted from 1900 to 2100, on the outskirts of Sharm al-Sheikh. As a result of the exercise, we established that the LAW rockets would be launched at a distance of 85 to 110 yards from the target.

THE COMPOSITION OF THE FORCE

The force that was assigned to carry out the fourth operation at Hurgada was comprised of the following men and means: *Snunit* #1 was manned by the author, who served as the mission's commander; Lieutenant Commander Gadi Sheffi, the commander of the force; Chief Petty Officer (Res.) David Kliot, the boat's operator; Petty Officer First Class Yochanan Sade, who operated the MAGs; and Petty Officer First Class Uri Stein, the LAW operator. This was the fourth time that Kliot was taking part in an operation at Hurgada. *Snunit* #2 bore First Lieutenant (Res.) Israel Dagai, the *Snunit*'s commander; Chief Petty Officer (Res.) Yair Michaeli, the boat's operator; Petty Officer First Class Rami Tzur, the MAG operator; and Petty Officer First Class Dani Eitan, the LAW operator. The rescue and backup team on board the third *Snunit* consisted of its commander, Rear Admiral (Res.) Yochai Ben-Nun; Chief Petty Officer (Res.) Itamar Levi, the boat's operator; and the team's MAG and RPG operators, Petty Officer First Class (Res.) Yair Selah and Petty Officer First Class Reuven Spitzer. A rescue helicopter, manned by Lieutenant Commander Eli Marek, stood on alert at Ophira Airport, but would only conduct missions outside the aerial missile-defended zone.

THE ROAD TO HURGADA

As soon as the second LAW missile exercise was over, we headed off to Hurgada. At 2200, after about an hour out at sea, one of the two engines on *Snunit* #2 malfunctioned off Shadwan Island. I thus ordered the crew to switch boats with the backup unit and asked Yochai Ben-Nun to return to Sharm al-Sheikh with the stuttering *Snunit*. The two remaining *Snuniyot* continued to the target at a slow pace through calm to choppy seas.

Over the course of the journey, we noticed the searchlight beams scanning the area of the installation from what appeared to be the southern part of the anchorage and eventually confirmed that the searchlight was indeed adjacent to the southern entrance. As established during the briefing, I gave the order to enter from the north and Gadi Sheffi set a new course. As such, we traced the coastline of the Giftun Shoal, heading north and then west, so that we eventually approached the target from the northeast, while scraping the surface of the reef.

DEVELOPMENTS AT THE TARGET

Upon entering the anchorage we found the entire harbor pitch dark with no sign of any movement. Consequently, Gadi Sheffi smelled a trap. Gadi suspected that the enemy troops were waiting for us to enter inside before lowering the boom. However, I responded that we were already inside the anchorage and that we would press on toward the target.

The force thus continued to make its way into the heart of the installation via the central passageway. We soon noticed a dim mass with blurry lines about nine hundred yards from us. The object was prominently positioned in the center of the anchorage, to the north of Minkar Island. Apparently still under the influence of the "trap hypothesis," Gadi Sheffi suggested that it was the capsized missile boat, which Gadi Kroll and Dan Uzieli had incapacitated during the second operation. I told him that we would nevertheless continue to advance until we managed to identify whether it was indeed the latter or the full profile of a missile boat. If it turned out to be the capsized boat, our *Snunit* would continue in the direction of the pier. Upon identifying the target, the second *Snunit* would cover us as we approached the missile boat, before joining the fray itself.

When the force was within about 450 yards of the blurry object, we realized that it was indeed a missile boat with a full profile. Consequently, the two *Snuniyot* edged closer with the objective of mounting the attack. The missile boat was ensconced behind the reef, which itself was covered by the high tide. As a result, the reef's borders were obfuscated (a point we realized only

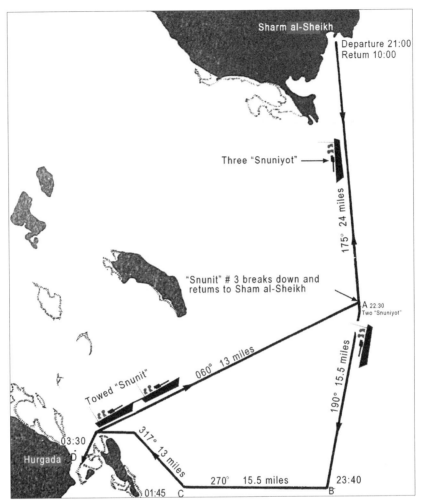

Movement of forces during Operation *Magbit* 16—Fourth attack (night of October 21–22, 1973).

after the fact). This clever "cover" was probably intended to prevent divers or explosive boats from engaging the target.

Upon reaching within 130 yards of the missile boat, we came under fire from a 23-mm automatic gun on the Giftun Shoal, to our left. The 23 mm was immediately joined by light-weapons fire from the shadowy missile boat across the way, but I nonetheless instructed Gadi to get within firing range.

Once the gap was reduced to about eighty-five yards, we opened our attack. Each sniper fired LAW rockets from a crouched position on the stern of

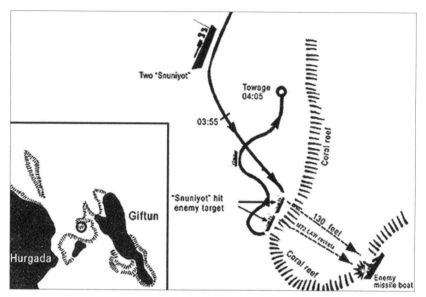

Operation *Magbit* 16—Outline of battle.

their respective boats, but the first six rockets—three apiece from each of the two *Snuniyot*—sailed harmlessly over the missile boat's mast. I thus ordered the crews to hold their fire and cut the distance to the target. We got within about forty yards of the target, but each of the *Snuniyot*'s fourth, and second to last, rockets were off the mark as well. At this point, I told Uri Stein, the sniper on our boat, that I would launch the final rocket myself. However, Uri managed to convince me that he was better trained than I was for the job at hand, and I handed over the rocket. Uri and Dani Eitan, the sniper on board *Snunit* #2, simultaneously launched their last rockets. This time around both LAWs found their mark and the missile boat went up in flames. As a result, the entire area was as bright as day. Egyptian soldiers, who jumped off the burning boat, were swimming all around us. Gadi fired the MAGs at the capsized Egyptians in an effort to fend them off and correspondingly sought to move the boat forward. However, much to our dismay, *Snunit* #1 was stuck on the reef.

It was already 0430, a mere thirty minutes before daybreak. I thus found myself mired in a difficult dilemma over whether to abandon ship—detonate our *Snunit* with the Gur charge and transfer the entire crew to the second boat—or attempt to extricate it from the reef in the half hour of dusk that remained. If we transferred to the second *Snunit*, the five extra passengers would weigh the craft down and we would be forced to crawl all the way back to Sharm al-Sheikh (a sixty-mile journey) at a snail's pace. On the other hand, if we managed to get off the reef, both *Snuniyot* would be able to burst out of the anchorage at full throttle. With this in mind, I decided to try and rescue the boat.

To begin with, we tried to lift up the propeller hubs to half length, which is one of the positions that the *Snunit* allows for. However, the propellers continued to scrape against the rigid surface of the reef and remained as firmly rooted as an anchor. I subsequently told Gadi that I would crawl to the bow in an effort to tip it downward with my body weight, so that the stern would seesaw upward. As I made my way across the deck, my foot bumped into the MAGs' electric activation button, which Gadi had forgotten to lock. This triggered a burst of fire from the two machine guns that convulsed the entire boat. My hands, which were holding on to the barrels of the machine guns on both sides of the deck for support, were scorched by the heat released from the MAGs. I continued to crawl in the direction of the bow, but the stern would not budge. Only then did I come up with the idea of having everyone, except for the boat's operator (David Kliot), jump onto the reef for the purpose of reducing the boat's weight. As soon as everyone jumped off, the stern swung up and the propellers were released. The entire crew felt a huge sense of relief as it pushed the boat off the reef and hopped back in, but it was not to last for long.

We finally got around to withdrawing at 0445, but the *Snunit* immediately began to zigzag. I excoriated Kliot for finding the time to pull stunts, but he insisted that he wasn't responsible for the boat's swerving. Kliot suggested that one of the propellers was probably damaged, so that the functioning propeller was skewing the boat's movement. In consequence, I ordered the second *Snunit* to pull up beside us and tie the damaged boat to its stern with a rope. *Snunit* #2 then dragged us all the way back to Sharm al-Sheikh at a speed of only ten knots.

As we headed for the exit of the anchorage, the 23-mm gun on Giftun continued to fire away at us, but none of the Egyptian defenders gave chase. We reached the exit at 0500, just as dawn was beginning to break over the horizon. Upon passing Shadwan Island at 0700, we received word that a cease-fire had been declared between Israel and Egypt. Three hours later, we were back in Sharm al-Sheikh.

RESULTS OF THE FOURTH ATTACK ON HURGADA

The fourth operation at Hurgada also attained its objective: an Egyptian missile boat was destroyed and our forces returned safely to base. As a result of the mission, the Egyptians withdrew all their naval vessels from Hurgada to Safaga, some thirty miles to the south.

The chief of the Navy's Intelligence Department informed me over the phone that the missile boat we destroyed had taken part in the sinking of the INS *Eilat* in 1967. I reminded the department chief that both events occurred on October 21–22, the same date as the sinking of the *Emir Faruk*, an Egyptian ship, during the War of Independence in 1948.

Much to our chagrin and despite the success of the fourth mission, Operation Ohr Yarok—one of the primary reasons that we attacked Hurgada four times and undertook to secure freedom of action at the entrance to the Gulf of Suez—was taken off the agenda.

At any rate, once the Egyptians evacuated the Hurgada Anchorage, the Red Sea Theater was able to transfer all its forces to the north. To wit: we participated in the navy's contribution to the capture of Port Adabiyah, evacuated the 1,500 Egyptian POWs from Adabiyah to Ras Sudr, and closed the siege on the Egyptian III Army by blocking it off from the sea; our LCTs combed the Gulf of Suez's shipping lanes for maritime mines; and we helped guarantee the continued flow of oil to Israel.

The Uniqueness of the Hurgada Operations and their Achievements

The operations at Hurgada Anchorage were carried out against a densely fortified frontline target that was crawling with guards. During the Yom Kippur War, the Shayetet-13 attacked the target four times within thirteen days of combat and penetrated the anchorage three times. Over the course of these operations, two of the four missile boats in the Egyptian ORBAT (order of battle) along the Red Sea front were destroyed and one of the installation's piers was ruined. In contrast, the IDF forces did not incur so much as a single loss.

The Shayetet's commandos had to reach the target from a considerable distance, as the IDF's closest launching base was in Sharm al-Sheikh, some sixty miles away. In no other sector did the Egyptians forces enjoy such a clear-cut advantage in the balance of power, particularly with respect to the naval dimension. In the absence of other alternatives—sea, land, or air—a small-scale special operation by naval commandos constituted the only means for launching an attack on Hurgada.

The S-13's operations at Hurgada ultimately compelled the enemy to evacuate its forces from the anchorage. This was an unprecedented step, which yielded valuable strategic dividends: the threat against Sharm al-Sheikh and on Israeli shipping at the entrance to the Gulf of Suez was vastly reduced; freedom of action was attained throughout the area; and the operations paved the way for the planned armored landing in the southwestern part of the Gulf.

Furthermore, the strikes against Hurgada proved that it was possible to produce strategic results by means of a "special operation." Each of the infiltrations of the anchorage transcended all of the IDF's previous "operational frameworks." For example, two of the missions were executed with weapon systems that were either inadequately tested (*Patzchanim*) or completely unfamiliar to us (LAW antitank rockets). If we had conducted an operational patrol of the target or, at the very least, a "model drill" before the war, our level of preparation for the raids would have been immeasurably higher. Nevertheless, the sophistication and array of methods and means that were devised and put into action, along with the timing that was chosen for the sake of catching the enemy off guard, enabled us to penetrate and pound the same heavily defended target time and again, until the enemy felt it had no choice but to evacuate the installation.

The extraordinary perseverance of the *lochamim* and the determination of the command echelon were the decisive factors that tipped the scales in our favor. Last but not least, all this was accomplished without suffering any losses at Hurgada whatsoever.

Notes

INTRODUCTION

1. Shayetet and S-13 are used interchangeably throughout the book.
2. The Palmach constituted the regular forces of the *yishuv* (the Jewish community in Mandatory Palestine) and subsequently formed the backbone of the fledgling IDF during the War of Independence.

CHAPTER 1. NAVY COMMANDO IN THE WAR OF ATTRITION

1. Mustafa Kabha, "Kharb al-Istinizaf—The War of Attrition from the Perspective of Egyptian Sources," (Doctoral thesis submitted to Tel-Aviv University, 1995), 30 [Hebrew].
2. Avraham Zohar, *The War of Attrition, June 1967–August 1970*. Temporary, History Department, General Staff, Agam-Training Doctrine, March 1998, p. 432 [Hebrew].
3. Ibid., 225.
4. Kabha, "Kharb al-Istinizaf," 35.
5. Zohar, *The War of Attrition*, 225.
6. A regular division, as opposed to a reserve division. In Israel, reserve units take an active role in the country's defense, even during times of peace.
7. A clandestine operation aims to maintain the secrecy of the mission even after it has been completed (e.g., a reconnaissance patrol), whereas a covert operation is only supposed to be surreptitious at the outset (e.g., a surprise infantry raid, where the crack of gunfire is bound to blow the force's cover).
8. Kabha, "Kharb al-Istinizaf," 6.
9. Ibid.

10. It is worth noting that the pigs were utilized in all three operations, be it as part of the actual mission or for advance recon patrols.

CHAPTER 2. THE RAID ON GREEN ISLAND

1. *Great Raids in History*, ed. Samuel A. Southworth (New York: Sarpedon Publishers, 1997).

2. *Bulmus 6—The Assault on Green Island, the Night of July 19–20, 1969*, Navy Headquarters, History Section, August 7, 1987, p. 75 [Hebrew].

3. The terms "grip" or "breaching force" and "first wave" refer to the S-13 troops that fought on Green Island. Each of the terms is used in accordance with the particular content and context.

4. If the Shayetet had had another twenty divers/operators at its disposal, we would have preferred to integrate them into the second wave instead of the Sayeret Matkal's commandos. The main reason for this was that swimmers could have initially deployed some two hundred yards from the target without being spotted. As soon as the breaching force began to cut the fence, the second wave could have joined them. This situation would have improved the degree of surreptitiousness and facilitated the efforts of the two waves to reach the island in succession.

5. This problem did not warrant enough attention during the SOP because the exercises were held in Atlit's bay, which is only about thirteen to sixteen feet deep. As a result, only three officers equipped themselves with depth gauges. Likewise, several individuals misjudged the impact of the excess weight on the submerged approach and took along extra ammunition at their own behest. The unexpected depths might have also compromised the insulation of our grenades.

6. The "grip area" refers to the expanse on top of the compound's northern wing, from the edge of the roof until the air intakes on its southern tip.

7. This was reminiscent of the raid against Adabiyah. Contrary to the intelligence from *Aman*, there was no radar at Adabiyah either, even though the entire outpost was dubbed a "radar station."

8. *Bulmus 6*, p. 7.

9. *The Raid on Green Island—The War of Attrition*, Internal paper of Training Base #1, January 1995, p. 28 [Hebrew].

10. Ibid., 86.

11. From an internal document of the Israeli Navy [Hebrew].

12. Until the Six Day War, France was one of Israel's primary arms suppliers.

13. Author's comment: For reasons of its own, the Sayeret Matkal was not

debriefed by the cadets in the Shayetet's company commanders course who conducted the study. However, the Sayeret's commandos participated in the debriefings that were held shortly after the operation, and the recordings of these interviews were at the disposal of the cadets when the study was conducted.

14. *Rashomon* is a film by the Japanese director Akira Kurosawa. The title of the movie has become synonymous with a situation in which it is difficult to glean the truth due to conflicting accounts by valid witnesses.

15. Flannelette is a cloth that IDF soldiers normally use to clean out the bore of their rifles.

CHAPTER 3. OPERATION ESCORT: THE SINKING OF TORPEDO BOATS IN THE GULF OF SUEZ

1. *Elul 14* was the date that I requested according to the Hebrew calendar. Unlike its Gregorian counterpart, the Hebrew year is predicated on the lunar cycle, and the moon is always at its fullest toward the middle of the month.

2. In Israel, young men are conscripted into the army and required to serve nearly three years in what is referred to as *sadir* (the regular army). Soldiers who wish to extend their service or pursue military careers enter the *tzva keva* (standing army).

3. The Israeli equivalent of earning a high school diploma.

4. At the outset, Senior Chief Petty Officer Aryeh Yitzchak (Aryo), a superb professional pigist, was assigned to this team, but he showed up late to the final operational briefing. As a result, and despite the objections of his immediate officers, I replaced him with the backup operator, Shmuel Tamir. In my estimation, strict adherence to every last word was essential to the mission's success.

5. Zero-in balance is a method for "gauging" and "balancing" a craft before setting off to sea. More specifically, the technical crew calibrates the pig's weight in the water and balances the bow and stern so that the vehicle sits parallel to the surface level of the water. This is the only position in which the pig can be duly controlled and its energy preserved in all modes of movement.

6. In the post-operation debriefing, Fatty referred to the difficulties he had accepting my order to descend into minimal buoyancy. "When I received the order," he said, "I banged on the table and screamed: 'What kind of an order is this?' But I carried it out because I had faith in you!" I responded

with the following words: "You simply internalized the importance of *discipline*, as the wireless silence that was imposed on us precluded both questions and the need to provide answers." In my estimation, Fatty's compliant response largely stemmed from my decision to replace Aryo for showing up late to the briefing for Escort 1. This disciplinary measure was intended, inter alia, to let the men know just how important it was to strictly adhere to orders, without any dithering or objections.

7. The first enemy military vessel to be damaged by means of limpet mines was the *Igris*, which was detonated on the night of November 29, 1948, while berthing in the port of Beirut. The mission was carried out by a lone commando, Eliyahu Reika—a graduate of the Palmach's Arab Department, who was given only scant rudimentary training before the mission. The ship that Eliyahu attacked was originally Hitler's cruising yacht, but was subsequently fitted with cannons and converted into an auxiliary craft for the German Navy. It was eventually purchased by a wealthy Lebanese with the intention of operating it within the framework of an Arab navy.

8. This was the standard limpet mine that was taken on maritime operations. The pig is a classified vehicle, so that if operators are forced to abandon the craft they can prevent it from falling into enemy hands by destroying the craft with a mine.

9. A health resort in Nahariya, a small coastal town in the western Galilee.

CHAPTER 4. THE S-13'S OPERATIONS AT THE HURGADA ANCHORAGE DURING THE YOM KIPPUR WAR

1. The brainchild behind Operation Ohr Yarok was the deputy chief of the General Staff, Major General Israel Tal ("Talik").

2. The *Tiran* tank is the Hebrew name for the Soviet T-54. The Israeli Army captured quite a few of these models during the Six Day War.

3. For a detailed account of the Egyptian Navy's deployment and its bases in the Red Sea during the Yom Kippur War, see: Rear Admiral Ashraf M. Refaat (Ret.), Egyptian Navy, "How the Egyptian Navy Fought the October War," U.S. Naval Institute *Proceedings*, (March 1995): 94–97.

4. Ibid.

5. An Air Force base in the Jezreal Valley, northeast of Haifa.

6. The offensive action was carried out by the Air Force because the latter had discontinued the practice of transporting pigs over the sea (*sketim*, trial) in the pylon of *Yasuhr* helicopters (Sikorsky SH-53) due to technical

reasons. Several months earlier, on the night of December 26–27, 1969, a *Yasuhr* whisked away a Russian radar in Operation Tarnegol (rooster) 53.

7. The construction of the latest version of the pig began during my tenure as the head of the Shayetet.

8. Although Shadwan Island was in the middle of the way, we had to keep our distance from the isle because of the strong likelihood of running into Egyptian forces.

9. *Snuniyot* is the plural form of *Snunit*. Depending on the gender, Hebrew plural words usually end in either "*im*" or "*ot.*"

10. Gadi Sheffi, the deputy commander of the Shayetet, Yedidya Ya'ari, and Yair Michaeli were among the veterans of the Shayetet's boat unit. Most importantly, the three were trained explosive boat operators. The last time the Shayetet used this type of boat was in July 1969, within the framework of the SOP for the raid on Green Island (the idea to utilize explosive boats at Green Island preceded the idea of positioning a holding detail on the maritime signpost by means of a pig).

11. During the Yom Kippur War, the Americans shuttled jet loads of equipment to Israel in order to replenish the IDF's dwindling supplies.

Index

About the Author

REAR ADMIRAL ZE'EV ALMOG was born in Tel Aviv, Israel, to parents who immigrated to Israel from Poland in 1933 and who lost most of their family during the Holocaust. He grew up in the city of Haifa. In 1952 he joined the Israeli military and served for thirty-three years, with his highest position being the Israeli Navy's commander in chief. Rear Admiral Almog volunteered for the Israeli Naval commando unit, Flotilla 13, in 1954 and served there as a warrior, an officer, and the unit's commander. He participated in five wars and hundreds of combat operations. Between 1986 and 1995 he was the CEO of the government-owned Israel Shipyards Ltd. and led a successful turnaround plan. In 1981 Rear Admiral Almog was awarded the Legion of Merit by the U.S. Secretary of Defense. He is a graduate of the Hebrew University in Jerusalem and the U.S. Naval War College. He is married to Dr. Geula Almog (children's literature expert) and is the father of three: Gal, CEO of a high-tech company; Oz, a professor of history and sociology at Haifa University; and Ram, CEO of a high-tech company. He has seven grandchildren.

The Naval Institute Press is the book-publishing arm of the U.S. Naval Institute, a private, nonprofit, membership society for sea service professionals and others who share an interest in naval and maritime affairs. Established in 1873 at the U.S. Naval Academy in Annapolis, Maryland, where its offices remain today, the Naval Institute has members worldwide.

Members of the Naval Institute support the education programs of the society and receive the influential monthly magazine *Proceedings* or the colorful bimonthly magazine *Naval History* and discounts on fine nautical prints and on ship and aircraft photos. They also have access to the transcripts of the Institute's Oral History Program and get discounted admission to any of the Institute-sponsored seminars offered around the country.

The Naval Institute's book-publishing program, begun in 1898 with basic guides to naval practices, has broadened its scope to include books of more general interest. Now the Naval Institute Press publishes about seventy titles each year, ranging from how-to books on boating and navigation to battle histories, biographies, ship and aircraft guides, and novels. Institute members receive significant discounts on the more than eight hundred Press books in print.

Full-time students are eligible for special half-price membership rates. Life memberships are also available.

For a free catalog describing Naval Institute Press books currently available, and for further information about joining the U.S. Naval Institute, please write to:

Member Services
U.S. NAVAL INSTITUTE
291 Wood Road
Annapolis, MD 21402-5034
Telephone: (800) 233-8764
Fax: (410) 571-1703
Web address: www.usni.org